Apples for Addicts and Alcoholics

Book I

James Page Jr.

To order additional copies of this book, contact:
Xlibris Corporation
1-888-795-4274
www.Xlibris.com
Orders@Xlibris.com
83342

CONTENTS

BOOK I

BOOK II

FORWARD

This book is all about spiritual upliftment and to get you to take a look at dealing with your problems with your spiritual eye as well. As faith comes fear goes, we are stepping on the toes of all our foes. We know that drugs and alcohol is not our friend, nor is stress and other mental illness. Life has many seasons to weather, how fast dark clouds and storms can form. Let change be the reason for the season. This book will help you to weather proof, I can't stand the rain, the heat and the cold gets old, so spring into action for summer, winter, spring or fall. Stand for something or fall for anything, I do not think it's in Gods plan for you to be the fallen Man/Woman. This book will feed your spirit!!!

INTRODUCTION

This book has been in the long time making. My name is James Oscar Page Jr, I am an Addict / Alcoholic and I approve this message. The message is that we can over come addiction with self-help and help of others. We will over come our self, spirit over flesh. This book will feed your spirit and your spirit will become as popeye over drugs and alcohol and the brutis life style. I have had all I can take an I am not taking no more, you will have it your way if you hear what I say, you do not need to see it but you must believe it, then you will achieve it. Going green, spinach words for your spirit gives you super soul power. First, I need you to know what my apples stand for and then you can stand with me. These apples will be for upliftment in life. APPLES stand for—All People Progress/Over Life's Evil Sins!!!! That's why we say apples for addicts and alcoholics. We will progress if we will to do so. In recovery, practice makes progress. You can make a difference in your life by practise. I have a desire to up lift people so I wish to start a movement that I need you to be a part of, each one of us do our part by spreading spinach words will be a big start. The movement is a vision of Apples For All. Again—Apples For All = All People Progress/Over Life's Evil Sins, Faith/In Our Rise, Almighty's Love Lasts. That's apples for all and it's a worthy cause, and will help you to help your self as well as help others. As Faith comes fear goes, and the brutis lifestyle we are stepping on their toes. We all have seasons in your life, let change be the reason for the season, life gets better when you weather proof. I can't stand the rain, the heat, the cold and storms get old, time to spring into action. Apples for all, that's my call. The things I have been though in life got me ready and I am set to go. Talk to your self, talk to your spiritual self, because in the beginning was the word. So let it be good words you feed your soul, as the saying goes food for thought. Each one teach one that life can be what we will it to be, set your spirit free and eat the good apples off the apple tree. Spiritually speaking, a good apple a day will keep the evil/bad things away. Stand for something are fall for anything, it is not in Gods plan for you to be the fallen Man/Woman, you are more than welcome to stand with this apples for all movement. As Jesus request for us to feed his sheep, read this and other self-help books and eat spinach words for your spirit to grow on.

TRANSFORMATION

Have you seen superman run into the phone booth and transform. Also the incredible hulk turn green and rip out of his clothes. We addicts think drugs and alcohol transform us into superior beings. We think we can socialize better, love better or even perform better. We love the thrill of the action. But even the hulk and superman are transformed for only a short period and then they go back to normal life. We never want to take off our addict suit. We see normal as boring, hurtful shameful and hopeless. The more we wear the suit the more out of touch we become with who we are. We need to learn who we are and not run from ourself, not be ashamed of ourself. Make up, wigs and perms cannot cover shame. We do not need to cover it, we need to uncover it and deal with it. Also when we wear an addict suit too much we become immune to it. When taking too much medicine the pills will not work and have the effect and power to cure now. Our body and mind now build an anti defense to the meds. Just the same when we drink and use drugs, we no longer get high or drunk on small amounts, we need more and more. Soon the mind needs and wants more but the body cannot deal with so much and we crash, overdose or burn out. Not even our superman suit can give us the power to deal with life. Covering up the hurt, the shame, the guilt only cause us to drink more, trying to drink the shame away. Who are you? You need to know who you are and what it takes to overcome the pain and shame. Work on loving you now. Find the superman in the normal man. He is asleep, wake him. Go green the right way, not hulk style change.

SINCE I MEET YOU

Since I met you life began to feel so strange. It seems I met myself for the very first time. Me meeting me, the sober me and the honest me, the real me. The spiritual man not the street or worldly man. The man that's willing to be about human love and soft core rather than hard core. The strong survive and the meek strive. Now this is new to me and new found life can be lived lamb like, not the black sheep, or the king lion. Now the lamb with my name in the book and the shepard watching my back while I graze on the grass that's supplied by the grace of God. When I get full and hot I have a barber to sheer me of this wool and some needy men is covered in this wool as I am covered in blood from above. I get to lay back and uncover myself of all this thick wool and thick skin. I get to uncover and get to know me without fear, without shame I get to know me and shepard approved. The stamp of approval is like a choice cut prime rib that feeds the need of hardworking men that protect and save and serve the most high of the high. When you know you are a part of something great yet little oh you know that you were raised for this moment and your place is important as well as valued and recognized by meaningful people too. When you see yourself and your purpose and the pride to be you, to be a man, to be an american, to be a father to your kids and a husband to your wife, to be a fan of the Vikings and just proud to be you. When the perfect peace shine in your heart and the world makes you proud to have had the honor and the grace God gave to you leave you feeling happiness that's not man made, not money or anything can give you this perfect peace and joy. This is the moment you met you and felt one with the father, son and holy higher power.

FOUR WALLS

Stuck inside these four walls. We lock our feelings up and put a wall around them. We do this for protection to keep people out, but we lock ourself in. We lock away our shameful feelings as well, we need to share feelings because this is how our spirit relates to God and other spiritual people. The wall hinders us from sharing true feelings and in turn we cannot have meaningful loving relationships. Stuck inside these four walls, sent inside forever. Never seeing no one nice again, like you. If I ever get out of here, I'm going to give it all away. When giving we receive and you can get out of your walls one brick at a time. Give away the shame and the guilt and resentments they will kill you. Also give away the love and get love in return. Prison walls are meant to hold people in for doing something bad, the walls are their punishment. A fence holds dogs in their yard and there are invisible fences. We have the invisible walls as well that holds in the bad habits we have, to hold in resentment is a self killer. Some walls are made to keep others out, and some are to keep others in. The wall does its job without thought of the effect or the time to open or close. We are the gate man of our wall and soul and we hide from issues that are confrontational for us. Face them down so we can grow with the rest of the world, with the changing times. Wall to wall if walls could talk, who knows what goes on behind closed doors. In Tampa they have a Laundromat with no walls. It has a top over it and a ground foundation but no walls. People still come and go and clean things they have. Bottom to the top or side to side, what's stored in you, open up and see, not for me, but to set your spirit free.

FLYING

What goes up must come down, except for God. An eagle soars but must come down to feed. An airplane must come down for maintenance and gas. We as addicts need to realize that we can not stay in the clouds, are as high as a kite. Have you ever had a coworker tell you to come back down to earth? They say that an unreasonable or unreachable person put themselves above, while a reasonable person is down to earth. That's where we live our life and relate and share with others. While it's great and necessary to have your spirit soar, but keep your ego here on earth. Much pride, much slide. Reach your brothers and sisters here on earth and God above. I heard a saying I like, Prayers go up and blessing come down. I do like that saying and believe in it. As far as recovery goes, it's important to keep the ego in check. Grandiose attitudes leads to dry drunk lifestyle. Misery loves company, and in my opinion we need to learn to have sober fun. That's one of the lies we told ourself that life was boring until the weekend with beers that start with the letter M. Then we wanted weekdays as weekends and beer anytime and all the time. Weekends are made for spring cleaning and even a days rest. For family time or others things we can think of. I did also hear a woman say she was scared to be inside her mind sober. That's too many a scary place to be and an uncharted place as well. Fear of the unknown maybe? You can fly and land in a place that's family friendly too. Try to know the real you without fear.

BODY AND SPIRIT

Body and soul as the old saying goes, it takes two. Not me and you but me and me see, body and soul. If all the things we learn about ourself, we learn we are made of two living parts, body and soul. We also learned that god is spirit and we pray in spirit as well. In the bible they say test the spirit. The body have needs such as food, water and love. It needs cleaning and washing and so on. The spirit has its needs as well, love, life lifting words is its food. The body has many lusts such as sex and human touch. It is hints that the spirit is greater than the body. The body is called the shell for the spirit. Just as a car has a body and a motor, then there are brakes, tires and so on. We have feet, hands and so. The two must both be taken care of to keep the value and worth up. Other hints out of the bible is greater is he that's in you than he that's in the world. We go to the mechanic shop to charge our battery and tune up our motor. Where do we go to charge our soul and tune up our spirit? Test your spirit. We relate to the world with our body and mind and intellect, but we relate to God in spirit, in faith, in prayer. IT TAKES TWO. Guard your heart and have faith.

A LOVELY DAY

A lovely day, a lovely day, today is a lovely day. Today is a great day to be sober and drug free. Today is a great day to be free from jail and drummer free as well. A good time to set personal goals and strive to reach them with all the access we have to great wealth. Yes a man with a plan or a woman in this time and area can reach heights that's whole villages could not reach in times gone by. The simple days are gone by, but today is a lovely day anyway. High speed internet, huge income, the world we live in today gives us power in our hands to do the unthinkable in this day and age. We have the power also in the spiritual world since the vast knowledge at our fingertips is so reachable. But truth comes with self awareness and strong family values and morals, and being selfless and God fearing people just like the old days minus old ways. Simple things like sitting at the dinner table as a family unit and united. It still comes down to inside rather than outside forces that gets the job done. Feeling, faith and works and self belief can move mountains of any size. Living in the day and one day at a time still fills the bill. Keeping it simple has its rewards as well. A fast moving world is not all it's cracked up to be and it can crack you up too. God grant me serenity to have a nice lovely day. Today keep the stress away and just slow it down today and feel all the inner peace and inner strength today that you can eat up. In this world and in this day have it your way just for today. Grace and thankfulness of life and the blessings it has to offer us today. Today and all days are what we make them. Make today a lovely day.

TODAY

Live for today because tomorrow is not promised to anyone. The only thing we have control over is today. Yesterday is gone and who knows about tomorrow? Living in the past or the future only takes away from today. Do your best today and it will help ease the let downs of the past. It will also open doors for a brighter future. And remember that you do not have to be perfect, just do your best. Your best is good enough, you do not have to be perfect. Thrive for progress rather than perfection. You are human and we all fall short of our Fathers glory. God help those who help themselves. Give us this day our daily bread. This day to shall pass. Why put off tomorrow what you can do today. PRAYER—Thank you Father for another day. When we do recovery one day at a time it gives us much more power in our lives. More control and not such a big picture to look at. Not look at being sober for the rest of our life long, but just for today, these 24 hours. It's like being in a boxing match and knowing one more round to get through. We can handle big things when they do not take on to much at one time. Little goals build us up for bigger goals. We are use to finishing things off and we gain more self confidence. Today we can stay sober.

GRATITUDE

A man was telling me a story of how he was walking down the street feeling sad for himself. He was sober or in a stage of dry drunk. Then he saw a man in a wheelchair and started to feel sorry for him, until he saw one crippled and blind. He now start to reflect on his own life and things to be grateful for. Now at that moment he went back to recovery again and not a sad dry drunk stage. Stinking thinking is not recovery. We have so much to be grateful for. At some point we were on the verge of losing everything, our spirit, hope loved ones and freedom. Today we have a chance of closing the door on the past road of destruction and despair. Have gratitude today for being sober. And have thanks for the new life you are now given. This little story is to make us aware that it's always someone worst off than we are. That is true too that we can look around us and find much to be thankful for. In material riches Minnesota is a wealthy state and the riches are very attainable for even the poor to live a fairly decent life compared to other states and cities. Other places in the world have poor care in hospitals to deal with issues from disease or wounds. We need to be thankful for what we have. Now we can work on our relationship with our higher power.

T.K.O.

I think I better let it go, it feels like another drug <t. k. o.> I am taking all the relapses and slips of a two time loser. It takes an alcoholic or addict to lose twice and start all over again. I tried to take control of drugs but they took control of me, I am drowning in this bottle fool can you not see. I need a four mirror wall around me and then maybe I can. In this drug and drinking world many fools have a college degree. It's a disease so none of that matter you see, not even status or race can save thee. No need to lose all hope, with sense you will see it's time to have a change of mind. I think I had better let it go, it's like stepping in the ring with Mike Tyson, its going to be a <t. k. o.>. PLEASE LET IT GO. With the help of the brother and sisters in A. A. or N. A. we can go the distance. Yes we can. Then it's no <T. K. O.> but a we can go!! It's no T. K. O. It's A. A. and we are now A Ok. The TKO is not worth the fight anymore. We are going for a straight KO of drug use and even more the life style that give kids the wrong message in our neighborhood. Tyson did not TKO anyone, he KO. Love TKO is the real big loss. We surely need to let it go, the drug TKO. TYSON being the knock out king, spoke of his drug treatment and the real life issues of losing his child. But he spoke out of a different corner or the other side of the fence. He seem to be at peace with his life now, and sure let it be known that money and its evil powers were not going to TKO him. He seem very strong of his plans and place in his life. He gave me clear ideals that his spiritual wealth was more important than the almighty dollar. This is a fight alright and we need to let drug use go. Just as getting hit up side the head has a long term affect, sure drinking and drugging has a deadly long term affect as well. Those fighters have trainers and coaches who can throw in the towel, we got sponsors and others to help see us though too. Use the tools and the people in your corner and you are a winner only when you retire totally from the ring of the circus and merry go round until you fall down. Champ get a key ring, its a N.A. thing.

TWO WAY STREET

I found the love of crack on a two way street and lost it on a lonely highway to prison. True love will never die so I been told. Crack love is not all what it's cracked up to be. Crack love is a lie and now I must cry it's final goodbye. That crack held me in desperation, I thought it was a relation until the evil of it shined its light on me. How could I be so blind to get hooked the very first time. To be fooled is a hurting thing, to be in love and fooled is a crying shame. I felt the blame, but addiction is a disease that forms in the brain and drives you insane. On two way streets are homes, love, family and friends. On that lonely high you can die anyway. You are going nowhere fast and headed for a head on crash. Drugs and a night out is like driving on the highway with your lights out. One way to hell or jail and it's no two ways about that. In the end it's Gods way or the highway. It's the right way or the highway. Now it's A calling on the streets for peace. Our streets are in our hands, but more important our lives are in our hands. We do not live our life for just us anymore, we strive to clean up our lives and be there for the new and up and coming younger people out here on these streets. The highway is a very lonely way of life, the drug world take too much out of our community. Its not a good feeling to lose loved ones to the streets. I found love on a two way street, now these highways and bi-ways and one ways have potholes, crack on the front and back, and there is nowhere to park at. Low riders smoked out with no driver because Cheech and Chong are both in the back, texting a dealer about the potholes. Take our streets back sober driver smoke free.

STOP

Do you love your alcohol, your meth, your weed, your crack and your heroin? Well you had better stop because it can be a life or death thing. The love you save may be your own, your headed for a danger zone <slow down>. The danger zone is addiction and/or alcoholism, <slow down>. You had better look both ways before you cross them 1st way is short term pleasure / the 2nd way is long term consequences. Look at it both ways and see if it is worth the misery crossing this danger zone. I say do not slow down, I say do not stop. I do say turn around / u turn! You turn around your life to save your life <stop>. Slow down on the fast living and stop the drugging and drinking. Save your love for the ones that love you. No love for drugs and/or the booze we use. Give your love to the ones that love you back. Hugs not drugs. S is for sobriety—T is for time in recovery—O is for oscar you are about to win for the best clean up act—P is for progress. But everyone can not win the oscar so your O will be for open and honest. O yes we can. By stopping you are about to get it going life/love comes from above. Respect the one that wore the glove. Look at the man in the mirror. Look at yourself and your drug use and your own Glove, if it don't fit you must quit. Stop. The life you save may be your own Do you use drugs for the thrill or the pain you feel? It does not matter what's the reason or the season, drugs kill. Legal or illegal who cares? I do so you slow down so you can stay around, stop. The life you save may be your own, stop. You are the apple of my eye, you will make me cry if you die, stop. STOP STOP STOP.

ONE TWO THREE

Lets do a silly one today, here we go. One two three do you want to be free? Well I'm telling you what you better not do. Do not get addicted to drugs or I am going to pull the rugs. You better hear what I say because I do not play. I am not play dough or play clay. I am drugs and I will take your life away. Crack, heroin and alcohol, we all will cause you to fall. I'm talking about the kind of fall that say I have fallen and can't get up. Help yelp you hear what I say? Now you will have to be in A. A. each and everyday. ONE TWO THREE DO YOU WANT TO BE FREE? Well you better listen to me. One, look out for number one, because two is not a winner and three no one remembers. ONE TWO THREE DO YOU WANT TO BE FREE? Then you better listen to me. One—one day at a time. One—one hit is all it took. One—a one hitter. One—one step or step one—admit we are powerless. ONE TWO THREE STAY DRUG FREE. One step, two steps, three free. One heart beat because your heart takes a beating. Two faced friends because with friends like those, who needs enemies. Three peat because playing against alcoholics the game is blacked out. One, two, three, do you want to be free? Stay off your feet and get on your knees. One two three, rock around the apple tree. The truth can set you free, but the truth be, one two three Jesus is he, that's right, the light. One apple tree, two unity, three community. One two three, our apple tree stands for unity in the community. One person can make a difference, two people can make a team, three can make a meeting, in life there is no cheating. You have to pay the cost, carry your own cross. You have no boss, make your own path in life and do not get lost. The Father, the Son, the Holy Ghost, one two three you can be free.

SHINING STAR

Shining star for you to see what your life can truly be. The old timers in A. A. or N. A. are like our shining stars. We don't look to model after the Hollywood stars, the shining stars are the ones who have found another way to live. We want to know what our lives can truly be without the use of alcohol and drugs. We need to know how to deal with life on life terms. Who better to show us than someone that has been in our shoes and understands the pain and struggle of addiction. Stars shine at night, so it's at dark times we need a shining star. Someone who has been in the darkness and found their way out. Let your light shine for someone. Shoe shine, you shine. Eyes shine, our time. Freaks come out at night and the nightlife is not the right life. But stars come shining through and they shine for me and you. Shine on, right on, shine on. Good living is not just for the stars, but the stars are for good living. You can be a star too, a star for the people that love you. A star for the new comer in your group. The boy or girl star that was born from the love of you. Let your star come shining through. How many stars are in the sky, I do not have a clue but its a special star up there just for you. Talking about stars, the gloved one is one of our biggest stars ever, but to fit in his shoes many of us have no clue. His spirit was a mystery to many. This world could not relate to much of his life. I do not know about his shoes but who could get in his socks. That's where it go with him socks not shoes, and shake his glove not his hand. Can you fit his shoes, what about his glove, if it don't fit you must quit judging.

GODS BEAUTIFUL CREATION

When people tell you to take the time and look at and enjoy Gods beautiful creation, we look at the flowers and things. But there is also the rainbows and fish and the sea. We have the clouds the bears and the horses as well. Have you ever seen a baby shorty after it's birth. God's most precious creation, so we are the product of Gods creation, in ourselves and our neighbor and all human beings. Do not just see another human and judge the beauty by the outer shell only, see the beauty in their eyes, action, words and deeds. See their personality, soul and spirit. What you see is what you get, see love get love, see hate get hate. Try to see God in everything because God is love!! I will tell you that I think we have a very beautiful city we live in here in Minneapolis. But America is the land of beauty from sea to shining sea. From the smallest of bees to the largest of mountains there is beauty to see, cars, boats and floats are man-made things. They all come out of the mind of man, which are from the spirit of God. The seasons change and cities are going green, which all bring out the beauty in nature. At state fairs and the zoo we see the birth of newborn animals, it holds us in wonder and amazement in the beauty of this process as well as the beauty of the fragile life. I like what I see, from leaves changing colors to them falling off the trees. It's all a sight to see and a man is nice to be, GOD WE THANK THEE.

SAVIOR

Sometimes we take on the role of savior. This puts pressure on us. Making us reach for perfection. Then once we fail and not measure up to savior or perfection, we lose confidence and self worth and take on a failure esteem. We cannot change anyone. Nor can we control anyone, but ourself. We can change our own behavior and thought pattern. No one can reach the perfection dream. It only put undo pressure on us. That takes on results that's counterproductive to our attentions and desire to help someone. We turn around and treat ourself worse than the person we are trying to save is doing to themselves. If we cannot save them join them type of thing. That's why in A. A. or N. A. they want the focus on you working on you. Also in recovery we lead by example, we model positive change. Most people can learn and follow what they see more than what they hear. If you talk the talk, you must walk the walk. When it's real love our family and friends feel they will follow on our heels. You will not have to worry about them keeping up because on your heels they will make you step up. Save yourself and it will be seen and felt and copied. SAVE SAVE SAVE, SAVE THE DAY ONE DAY AT A TIME!! When we think of saving someone, we think the enemy is outside of them, or outside of us. Not so much, we all need to be saved from self, and that's why its important to know the enemy we are at war with. It's not against flesh and blood, but the mind. God's armor, is the shield of faith and the sword which is the word of God. We must watch the words we put in our minds, our spirits.

RELATIONSHIPS

In this program of the 12 steps we recommend you not get into a new relationship in your first year of recovery. This is important or they would not be so firm on this. It's so that you learn to have a relationship with yourself. You can take inventory of yourself. You can get to know you without the mood altering chemicals. You can listen to your spirit and learn to trust its guidance. You can reclaim your values and know what makes you happy. Get back in touch with your passion. The most important relationship is the one with God. The second one is the one with yourself. Then wife, kids, family, friends or even pets. Once you are clear about you, it will become clear of these choices. A good prayer for us is to have a good relationship with God. In our first year of recovery we do need to start relationships but not a intimate one where sex is a part of it. It would require too much commitment and feelings that could take the focus off your recovery. This is a time for change and a time for self awareness. This is a time for self renewal and self uplifting. Not self pity or a reason to slack off ourself, but rather a time get a hold of our lives and get rid of deadly spirits in our lives.

RED NOSE

Like the story of Rudolf the red nose reindeer, we in recovery can see ourself that way. This is how we relate, his nose made him different and others made fun of him and thougth less of him. Our addiction puts a red nose on us. Like one foggy x-mas eve, we addicts and alcoholics have many many foggy days and nights the storms will come. But the fellowship can use you to guide another sufferer's sled. From meeting to meeting, delivering the message of hope, love and experience as a present freely given. The very thing in your addiction turn around and become good for others and now they no longer make fun of it. On the island of misfits only other addicts can reach them and place them with hope and love some where they are needed. Rudolf was on a mission with purpose to find his family lost in the snowstorm, that's when his big turn around came when he had a mission bigger than himself. He found others that had issues and together their determination mission accomplished. Not even the snow monster could stop this faith driven mission. Many others were helped as well, the family, the misfit, Santa and all. Look at what is possible when we do the right thing for the right reason. His compassion to not put others in harms way, but a real friend will help you see things through, the dentist and the gold man. The doe song to his spirit, "It's always tomorrow for dreams to come true" that's true for me and for you too. He went back for the misfits and love was the reason in the season. We are useful to other addicts and people who suffer from low self worth, we spread hope for them to cope.

LOVE IS LOVE

Love is a great gift! But love can sometimes hurt and leave us afraid to love. Have you heard the saying guard your heart? That does not mean build a wall and stop loving. It means do not let it turn hard or cold. To learn to love others we must learn to love ourself. When you treat yourself with love, others will find it easy to trust and respect you. Do not be full of yourself, that's not self love. It is a very big difference in self love and selfishness. Who is your worst critic, who treated you worst than anyone else. YOU DID YOU!!! So when you learn to take it easy on you and love you, that opens the door to spread that around. Mind, body and soul needs your love, you are now 100% ready to share your love. That's something the world is in need of LOVE. If you ever wonder what you can do for the world, there you go, the world is in need of love and that's something we all have to give. Many things in life now have been rooted in fear which cause walls to be built up for protection. The thing is that when one door closes we hope for hopes sake that there is another open door. Fear kills faith, but faith builds love. Faith is the glue that holds many things together, including love. Love is the thing that holds people together. Money makes the world go around. But it only turns it one way, and that's the way to get more and more. Love makes the world go around, but it has turns twists and moves that go round and round, up and down, back and forth. The things we do for love, at times we can not understand it, it's the most important commandment. Use love as a tool to teach the golden rule. Love is not fools gold, carry your load.

QUIET VOICE

Its a voice inside of you that will guide you if you can learn to listen to it. We are a physical and a spiritual person. The psychical person speaks loud and the words are formed in the mind out of the mouth to the ears of all who will listen. The spiritual voice do not come out of the mind, it come from the heart. This can't be heard but rather felt by others. You can feel it as well. We must learn to listen to it and also be guided by it. In a fast life style they say this is bad. But love is great, its a gift from god. Listen to your spiritual voice, God is spirit, I pray Lord help me to listen to my inner voice. The thing is that change is hard, but we can make it some what easier by thinking opposite of the way we learned to survive in the street life or the rat race of the material world. An example is as boys learning to be tough in the neighborhood we are told that having a heart was a sign of weakness. That was burned into our head and there were times the results would prove that their teaching was right. It would feel ego and muncho good, but I always had a little frizzy of a tickle run though my nerves. The show off rewards was only there around the guys, but do this alone and the feel you get is not at all a reward. Its a sting to your emotions. To compare the no heart jerk act, to being the guy that stand up for the victim you get a feeling that you have done the honorable thing. To me that is like superman coming to the aid of a needy person. All of us can be a super man when we listen to that quiet inner voice and be lead by it rather than the norm in basic situations. Wonder woman that go for you too, and the president too.

THE OZ

There will be tornadoes in your life, like Dorothy in the wizard of oz. When we alcoholic and addicts get sucked up into our addiction and in foreign places we should not be, lets do as Dorothy did. Her goal was to get back home. She needed help and had to go to the emerald city. She met other suffers along the way, and they shared their stories and charter defects and fears, No heart, no courage, no brains and no spirit to live. Together they walked down the yellow brick road with something in common, looking for life, hope and healing. That's the A. A. way. We can say Emerald city is our home group and the wizard is our sponsor. That's your A. A. home, but get back to your family because there's no place like home. A house is not a home <a home is where love is grown. In our lives the foundation in our homes need to rooted with love and strong family values, so we can weather the storms that life will throw our way. The winds of change will blow our way, if you are living its hard to stay out of the way of life happening. Even if you are in the safety of your home there is the chance of rain, fire or wind huffing and puffing and blowing your peace down. The twists and turns are lessons to be learned and the learning should start at home. Dorothy was not out in the big world alone, she had her dog total with her, and total was part of her family. She was not alone because her family love was with her in her heart. That's why she had such a strong need and want to get back home. She had the ability to bring the others together and they all worked at getting their needs met. Together they could do what one could not do alone.

ON THE ROAD AGAIN!!!

I can't wait to get on the road again. Road to recovery. We can be on a different road today. Not that road that leads to jails, institutions and death. Its a better road that leads to recovery, stability and life. We have been on this road before and I can not wait to get on that road again. Its a fork in the road. Turn around your life. I can't wait to get on the road again, making meeting with my friends, I can't wait to get on the road again. Life is a two way street, which road will you take? Its changes on the road all the time, the speed limit or a stop sign. We want the road to change. We need the change to happen on the inside. The fast lane can take you no where fast, but it is a road to recovery. Slow down take it easy. Easy does it. Do not be a road hog. Be a role model. Take off a load that old road is closed. Yes its my way or the hi way, we live sober today!!!!! Life is a long and winding road, it does not have to be a dirt road, how about the road to redemption. The yellow brick road or the road to grand mama house. Now the road to the heart of the ones that hold the keys to heaven, book me on that road trip that leads to eternal life. On the road to Adam's garden or to Eden house. On the road to recovery, yes, on the road again, I can't wait to get on the road again making meeting with my friends, I can't wait to get on the road again.

HOLD ON

I Will keep holding on, not hanging on but holding on. I wasted all those years and all those tears, but I will keep holding on. I will hold on to the new way of life I now have. The new freedom I have found, yes I will be holding on to that with both hands and all my might, I will hold on with my heart. The new peace of heart, mind and/or spirit. The new friends and members in the groups I attend. I will keep holding on to the hope I have found and the faith that got me more in touch with god. I will hold on to these new feelings that use to frighten me. I will hold on to my sobriety. I will hold on to my love ones. I will hold on to my understanding of my higher power. I will hold on to practicing these principles in all my affairs. I will let go of old ways and reach for the promises that we can look for in A. A. Although I already see them coming to play in my life. The rude awakings are so inspiring to me, now hold on with a purpose, with confidence and great expectations. I feel in doing so its a show thing that show others a difference and a reason to set goals, I like being a model for positive change to someone. I have been a giver in my life, but when living in negativity, it was not such good deeds I would give out. You can be a leader and lead people down the wrong path. So I feel I need to turn my life around for myself and for others as well. I would hope to do gods work as much as I did the devils work in the past. Blind, dumb and in the haze of drunken and drug poison state of mind can make a person drop his morals and do things they would not do in a sober mind state. Try it again and do it right this time for the good of God and his sheep.

I THINK I CAN

Its been said that if you think you can not do something, 99 % of the time you will not do it. On the flip side when you think you can, then half the battle is won already. In the story of the little old out dated train, it was his thinking that enabled him to pull the steep hill. After being down and out, used and abused, pushed aside, replaced and rejected, he stood up and took it one hill at a time. Self talk is so important. Why compare your self to all the new speedy trains and beat your self up. We are harder on our self than any others. What we think and tell ourself can change our day and our life. Our thinking can make a hill look like a mountain or the other way around if we are thinking positive. I THINK I CAN, I THINK I CAN!!! Better yet I think you can as well. Can we? Yes we can!!!! Affirmation is such a great tool. Get in the mirror and talk yourself into being what you will to be. You can do great things / the sober you that is. Pull your train of thought out of the station and take that hill because you are now sober and king of the hill or queen on top of the mountain. To reach the mountain top the stinking thinking must stop. Nothing can stop you if you put it in your mind, its mind over matter, and it matters if you think you can do something. I think I can safely say that you can think your way though any task. Positive thinking is better than any wonder drug. If you think you can, then I know you can, you can turn your life around and you can stay sober. The mind is a powerful tool and we were given the choice to chose, why lose, just follow the rules and think things though.

NO REASON

Give me just one reason to stay in a using drug world and I will turn right back around. All you drug dealers and drug users, I got your number and I know you got mines, I called you many times. I do not want any one to squeeze me that may take my life away. A spiritual heart can love you and give you what you need. I am to old to go chasing you now drugs and waste my precious energy, any way I know you want to kill me and there is not no more to say. Recovery saves lives and using drugs takes lives away. So do not think you have a reason to go back to your using life, its not one reason to go back. Who needs the misery that go with that life style, its not just the drugs but that world takes on a life of its on and its full of hate and cut throat jealous petty acts. No building any one up but all tearing each other down. Your using friends they only use you. Knives in your back yes its just like that, they got rules but no one follow though. Morals on the ground, morals on the ground, looking like a drunk with your morals on the ground. Hat turn south with a pipe in your mouth, its time to drop that hat and reach in your heart where your values are at. Recovering addicts are the best pound for pound, its time to get our morals off the ground. Reach in your heart where your values are at, straighten out your hat and straighten out your life, let your morals come shining though, life can be great and you are the living proof. I am on this side of the fence to stay unless you give me one reason and I will turn right back around. I do not think that will happen and I will try to keep my morals off the ground. No reason!!!!!! Not one, not one reason to turn back around, and not one reason to drop our morals on the ground.

ON THE MOVE

Ain't no stopping us now we are on the move. In this song title they talk about us and we, not I. Anyway we have some churches that's on the move, they are on fire doing gods work and helping people. Many groups are now coming together for a common purpose of serving the needy and helping others. I admire the way people put on pink and walk to get the word out, we do understand that people that has been through the same same make great supporters, or if your love ones has been affected, you also make great helpers. Just as in alcoholism or addiction, are diseases effects others. We all come together and support one another. But when a person has been in your shoes they make great helpers. Addicts helping addicts and alcoholic helping alcoholic. We can spot homeless and say they need help, they can see the outside of you and see the need. But people have things inside such as mental illness and disease of addiction, those problems are not seen or understood sometimes, but they can affect afamily and community. Lets get on the move and let nothing stop us, lets do what we are called to do. Visit, feed, and comfort the needy. People talk about big bother and the eye in the sky, but god is watching and a day comes when he tell us that he saw our deeds, good or bad. What's in your heart to do for the needy? What's your call to duty. Who can you hear calling, the army, the almighty, the neighborhood watch group, the school program, the internet watch police. Who is calling you, will you show up. Show up, not show out. Get up not give up. Give to not give in. Every little bit counts and helps. A small part is a big part. Do your part because it ain't no stopping us now we are on the move. We are moving mountains of problems out of our way, make way. God has a will and where there is a will there is a away. We take life day by day.

ON STAGE

Are you a movie star? Its been said that addictive people view their life as a movie. Its as if we are on stage at all times and acting. We lose touch with our real lives and who we are. We no longer play the father role in our family but rather the drunks' role at the bar. The movie become real to us and what's sad is we are the producer, star actor and director, but yet we play the saddest roles. We switch from role to role. One hour we are great on false pride and then superior with perfection, then comes the victim role, and after the poor me pity party we again go back to the captain of the team. Are you playing the star victim in your own movie? We need to know that day to day and even hour to hour our feeling change. All these treatment words like inventory seem corny, but to get real we must use the things that look fake and take and make the best out of them. No longer worry about what the others think and feel as far as you getting the tools to use that will help take you out side of the normal in your life. Hey do something strange for change in your life, get outside of your comfort zone and get in the zone. This is the real deal and a chance to turn the tables on your obstacle in your life, now. If you are the director in your life then you hold the cords to do you as you need to come out in your break out role. Time is not going to stop so its time to get off stage and on the red carpet. What speech will you give when you go up to accept the win trophy oscar or best something. Do it in your group at your support group, thank them and know to say I could not do it without, a whole village and higher power and family and so on and so many. One monkey don't stop no show, but one no show can affect the way our kids grow. One can be for given, two makes some question their reason for living, three you are picking the wrong apples off the tree, now a piece of their spirit is surely dying, what's your reason for lying. These things will now show in their show. Know that the lights and camera is on you, so take the right action to give your kids a star role in their own movie, thus and plus, it help us too. Even if your life is blue, stay true to the ones that love you, go green but stand on the red and do not let it go to your head, because you can get squashed like a bug and they will pull the rug. Its your life, but the lives of our love ones we cheer us on, so do not be afraid to share the stage, I love my oscar and your oscar too. Red carpet and red apple, be a good example.

LOOK INSIDE

We look for beauty outside of our self. We look for happiness out side of our self. We look for approval out side our self. We look at our outer appearance. All these things need to be ok on the inside before the out side. Who you are is not how you look. You can be a good looking ugly person. You can people please for approval, but if you do not approve of your self you will have no self esteem. Be grateful for who you are < not just what you are>. When we are kids people ask what we want to be, we struggle to learn who we are. You will gain more value by knowing who you are than how you look. Looks can open doors, but you are accepted by who you are. With age you can lose your good looks, with drug use you can lose your values. PRAYER Lord help me grow as a person and give me inner beauty.

JACK AND JILL

Jack and Jill went up the hill to fetch a jug of whiskey, jack fell down and broke his crown and Jill came stumbling after. When we look to alcohol or drugs to make our relationships more fun and bearable, they end up all broken up. We stumble through life in a drunken haze and simple things seen like a maze, in order to wake up out of this daze, try a sober mind and you will be amazed and even strangers will sing your praise. Jack and Jill in their thirst for the mood altering substance they ran up the hill. For your program of recovery will you at least walk up the hill. Easy does it, we can climb over any mountain of trouble. Now no longer follow jack to unhealthy places, stick with the winners. Because if you keep falling down you may break your crown or worst you could break your spirit. Jack is a person, the hill is a place and the bottle is a thing. Listen jack and Jill, also betty and bill, be carful of the people places and things in your life. If you break a bone after fallen down, push life alert, if you fall from grace and break your spirit, you should call on the holy spirit, or god or your higher power, or what or whom you believe in. The program works if you work it, find out what works for you and get to work. Regardless of the fall you can stand tall.

INSIDE JOB

Laughing on the outside, crying on the inside, the tools of A.A. have been used and tried. To get your recovery moving then our tools you need to be chosen because they are tried and proven. When we are feeding our flesh its desires such things as lust, greed, sex and other fleshly desires we seem to have it made. We feel we are happy, but on the inside we are crying. Our soul is left alone and the spirit cries to be loved. You know like the tears of a clown when there is no one around. All the big smiles and laughs and people think you are cool and jolly. But around them you focus on them and not your own emotions. When we are alone with ourself the flesh say run get sex, you can not be alone with your self or you will be sad, bored and very depressed. Run get drugs or alcohol or a sex partner, feed your flesh some mess or the spirit will get at you in the quiet peaceful times. The spirit needs food as well as the flesh and which one you feed is the one that will rule in your life. We must clean house inside out, we can not store in the shed deadly emotions such as anger, self pity, depression and the likes. We need stored at a arms reach, faith, hope and love. When we worry we are not walking in faith. A hunger spirit results in spiritual deadness. Emotions can be painful but we must not run from them, when we do not face emotions they turn into self defeating parasites. Parasites as worry anger, self pity and depression. We in turn cover these with drug and alcohol use, we allow these parasites free access at our heart and soul. Feed the one that you chose to rule your life. Are you lead by your flesh or by your spirit? WHY?

WIN OR LOSE

It's like flipping a coin, you will get either heads or tails. So take a chance because once you make the attempt you have a 50% chance to win or lose, succeed or fail. In life the big known fact is that your biggest loss is to not try at all. When we take on a task, if we do not win, that does not mean that we lose. You gain so much strength and knowledge along the way. We apply ourself rather than sitting around idle. There is another rule and it is a big one, if you use you lose. If you use drugs you lose the ability to have a sane serene life. Do you want to win or lose? It's a popular saying for people with confidence and egos that say we can not lose with the stuff we use. I say good! Its written that if God is for us then who can be against us. When God uses you then you cannot lose. But you have to serve Gods will for you more so than the will of yourself. Some losses can be used for the glory of God. The lessons we learn can be valuable, not taking risks can be costly. Taking risks can be costly also. The things in life that make you a winner depends on you and where you are in life, what's important to you in your life. No one defines your happiness for you. We do not follow the beaten trail. We blaze the trail that enables us to feel a purpose in our life that's family core and roots. Who are we and who are you. What makes us happy, who makes us happy. Success is what makes us have self worth and also success is when we give love to our family and raise them healthy and happy with morals and respect for the Lord above. That is mines, what is yours?

SUN SHINE BLUE SKY

This song was a hit. Sun shine blue skies please go away, my girl has found another and gone away. With her went my future, my life is full of gloom so day after day I stay locked up in my room. I know this may sound strange but I wish it would rain, cause rain drops behind my tear drops and no one would ever know that I am crying to go out side. I have to cry because crying ease the pain. The hurt I feel inside I refuse to explain, I just wish it would rain. This is a self defeating message in the world of recovery. but a great song. The recovery life works different then normal life. We can not blame a girl, nor give someone the power over our future. Nor can we hide from pain and hurt. We must get it out In the open. We drown our hurt in wine or drugs. We can not isolate. Real men do cry. We have groups of people shoulder to cry on as well. This may sound strange, but it feel super great. Feeling are thus things we must deal with in the recovery world. Not just the physical pain only but also the emotional feelings too. This disease on alcoholism and drug addiction really gives us a leg up on all sorts of other trouble on how to deal with them. Our recovery of this prepares us to deal with issues over and over again in life. We have weakness but the out come of dealing with them makes us strong in life. Also mind, body and soul we learn spiritual lessons in our fight to have sobriety. Which means having a sound serene life. Relationships and all meaningful things in life we are better prepared to deal with.

5th STEP

The 5th step can be taken many ways, pastor or sponsor. None of that is the big deal, the big deal is that you get naked of secrets in your life that hunt and hurt you. Its like cleaning out the fridge of old food and making room for fresh health food. Expose your self to your self. We are only as sick as our secrets. You can dress your self up in new clothes and cover up ugly issues, hiding and hurting us. Clothes do not make us no where near as much as the things we cover up. The way we feel about ourself can surely affect the way we act in life and the things we are willing to try to do in our lives and the things we will accept as treatment from others. That's why I feel the 5th step is one that's very important, but they all are. The 5th is one that we must be ready to take at the right time. In court when you do not want to hurt your self or someone else you plead the 5th. In court the 5th means you do not talk, in A.A. the 5th you do not hold anything back. In court you plead the 5th, in A.A. we plead that you take the 5th. In the world of recovery the truth helps, not hurt. The things that we did when we were low in spirit and using drugs or drinking, did not line up with our morals and values. That can hunt and stunt our growth. The 5th step is not a step to make us feel bad about ourself, its not a pity party or poor me or bad me session, its to clear our conscience so we can move on in life without an anchor of guilt holding us down. Let go and let god, give it to god. He sent his to take away or sins so we could get close to him. They are covered in blood not shame or the blame game. Let go and lets go. Hi 5, you or alive.

WITH OR WITHOUT

Its only two ways to live, with or without your heart. In my drug using life I trusted no one with my heart. Not even my own choices. A wall was built to shut my heart in and all others out. To deal with loneliness I used drugs and drank. My heart became cold and hard as necessary to make it in the street life. But the well spring of life flow though our heart. With a stone cold heart its not easy to get near to god or be Christ like. Live in the drug and street world without your heart < but in the sober and recovery world we need a heart. The greatest gift from god is love. Your heart must be open to love to do the will of god. You can have knowledge, faith or understanding, but without love you have nothing. HAVE A HEART!!! A story of a bully talk about a person and their heart. Some young kids was having problems with a bully and they all talked about it, they came up with the fact that he beat up and took the boys money, but the girls he melted and gave it all way to them. He did not have a heart when it came to the boys and when it came to the girls his heart just melted. Their plan to comfort him and expose his toughness and his weakness gave him a chance to even his standing. And they found out it was fear of love and not being loved that lead to his actions. And to be able to take a look at this in a non threating way helped him to look at this and his feeling and others feeling. Happy ending, he got a girl and a few friends. We use our heart any way so we may as well face fear and realize that others have a heart and feelings as well. We can not use it with girls and not boys, with blacks and not whites. Whole not half a heart.

HUMBLE

Do not try to lift your self above others. yes you want to lift your self but not for reasons to be over others. When we do it that way and for those reasons we step on toes < and then the same people we see going up we see them coming down. Let god lift you and then we do not step on toes, when we do it for his honor rather than our own honor, there is then no back lash. When we step on toes there seem to be many stumbling blocks along the way. Do not try to be the best player on the team but the best team player. I feel its better to seek to be humble rather than seeking honor. Let god do it for his honor and his glory. God grace is great, when he use you, you to help others, you are helping your self as well as god helping you too. This is a case of what goes around comes around, what you give out you get back. Have you ever heard that you can not out give god? Just as in the twelve steps spiritual program, carrying the message is a thing that fulfill many many rewards for both the giver and the receiver. H and H humble and honor, both makes the world a better place to live.

GOLD FISH

Environment is a major influence. To give yourself a extra chance at winning, you should hang around the winners. If you hang around active users then its more likely for you to use, or at least you will see so much dysfunctional behavior that has the effect of rubbing off on you. This can stunt your growth in recovery. You need to grow in recovery. Not just be sober. In order to see and receive the promise of A.A. or N.A., you must place yourself in the surrounding of people who lift your spirit rather than abuse your spirit. Gold fish in a small bowl will stay small, but put them in a huge tank and they grow much larger. PRAYER—Lord lead me to places that will help me grow. We can not fail in the spiritual world, but in environment failure is lurking at every turn. To compare to others and use their misery to succeed for self is a common thing in that world. The spirit world is a different world, and the ghetto world is a different world. The content of life is draining and despair is the norm, hopeless began to form and life become full of storms. Yes its a different world where we come from and environment can hold you down if inside of you faith is not found. Your spirit can rise and soar in a different world where failure can not touch you any more. Gold fish look good in a bowl but their soul can use much much more when it comes time to soar.

FOOL PROOF

What a fool believes. The wise man has the power to reason away. According to the words in this song you can be a wise man and yet still be a fool. What a fool believes, he think he can do the same thing and get different results. A wise man can come up with many reasons to be a fool, reason away. We also call this rationalizing or interlectionalizing. A wise man think he can figure out his own program, rather than do the program that works. Is that a fool are wise man? Being a wise man can think his way out of a rut, as well as think his way into a rut too. My best thinking got me in the jam I am in now in life. A fool thinks he is working the program by working ten steps when its a 12 step program. You believe the program works, well people that still use and want to quit believe it works to. Faith and belief without works and action is useless. Sometimes we need to think with our heart leading the way, or at other times or mind must lead the way. Trust both but know which leader are you in need of, spiritual or mental? The human spirit is powerful, as is the human mind. Look at where the mind has taken us since the cave man and jungle tribes, to the moon and driving, flying and all that from horse and buggy to trains and plains. That's the mind power, but the spirit power has taken us from slavery to reaching for one world order and the search for peace on earth and the golden rule and the most important commandment. We strive to reach gods vision for man kind though the love of a godly spirit. Gods plan for man is fool proof.

THE BRICK WALL

Walls are built to keep others out. The german wall did fall, the human will and togetherness did away with that. The great wall of china is big and long. But the wall we addicts build is a killer, going to N. A. or A. A. we can tear the wall down one brick at a time or one meeting at a time. Words are sharper than a two edge sword and many times at meetings I lose a brick off my wall. This wall do not have to fall, as bricks are removed it makes an opening. We need to be open so the sun can shine in our lives. When I hear something from a member at a meeting that I can relate to or agree with, I can program that into my brain, therefore changing my mind on thought at a time as well. Brick wall you will fall!!! People in A. A. have a lot to say. They will huff and puff and blow your wall down. We do not need no humpty dumptys sitting on us. All of A. A. women and all of N. A. men forget about humpty, help me do this wall in. What goes up must come down, I want to hear a loud cheering sound when this wall fall down. Loving spirit up and jailing wall down. No more hiding behind a wall, I want to share my love with all of y'all. Its the end and the beginning. Ain't no wall tall enough or wide enough to keep me from you.!!! Its time to do what we were put on this earth to do and that's let our love come shining though. Its a campaign against world hunger, I want one against love hunger too. Love hurts but lack of love is worst. A. A. and N. A. is like a brick house mighty mighty just letting it all hang out. Wipe out. No wall is to tall.

FAITH

When I started back in church my pastor had me read the faith charter in Hebrew 11. The main message there was <without faith it is impossible to please god>. Fear is the opposite of faith. Fear is a faith killer and faith kills fear. They can not live together. Alcoholics and addicts operate out of a lot of fear. Fear of pain, fear of hurting from loving. fear of trust, fear of being alone. Faith made Abraham offer his son as a sacrifice to god. In turn god blessed him with many seeds, he became the father of faith. We need to have faith in the program and people that wants to help us. In our self, god, a higher power, we need to have faith. Pray and practice to strengthen our faith. Man oh man with the faith of a mustard seed we can move mountains. And with faith we can please god and faith is free. Its with in us and with our eyes on the prize we can surely muster up the faith we need to please god. The prize is not drugs are things, not money. The prize is our spirit serving god, not our will but gods will. With faith and serving gods will for us, we will not have our eyes on our wants needs or problems, but on others people problems. Not o. p. p. other people property, but other people problems.

DEAD OR ALIVE

Lets talk about a dead spirit or one that's full of life. Your spirit lives within but its many many signs on the out side that tells the state of your spirit. Its life before death so we will speak on the life first. Your skin is a sign, its complexion and tone. Its smoothness and elasticity. a deaden spirit would result in skin of blotches, dry in areas and oily sweaty in some or brittle and peeling. The eyes of a live spirit would be shiny, bright, sparkly and reflective. Dead spirit eyes are lifeless, dull, flat and cold. You can also tell the condition of spirits most times in a person's walk, talk attitude and surely their actions toward others. The choice of life and death is yours. We always have a choice. Feed your spirit for life, live until you die. Because life keeps on slipping into the future. I want to fly like a eagle, let my spirit carry me. When an eagle fly its a symbol of freedom. Its like serenity soaring. But to let your spirit carry you is the most peaceful flight you will ever take. In the cartoons when a person dies their spirit takes off out of their body upward bound. Your spirit is the powerful part of you, its the life of you. You know you can have a false spirit, just as you can have false courage and false pride. You can drink your spirit, courage or pride out of a bottle. all are inside of you. Love, pride, courage. You must find them, trust them and nourish them. Its inside. What do it take to bring that out of you? Hang around people that inspire you and build off that. Conceive, Believe and Achieve your dreams. Set goals and go after them, lead and guided by your spirit. Go after them as if your life depends on them.

HOW YOU FEEL

How you feel will reflect in your actions, appearance, conversation, even in your eyes. Everything flows from the inside out, rather than things out to in. If you get depressed about something it still comes from inside out. When something happen on the out side thats bad or hard to deal with, that do not depress you. Its how you view it and feel about it that turns into depression. On the same token when you are pleased and happy about something, its the view and feelings as well. Its why we must keep major attention to our feelings. Feelings are the root to our recovery, if we manage them properly and challenge our belief system, we can deal with other issues more affective. Feeling, how many of us have them, feelings ones we can depend on. Feelings is something we use every day, but most of the time we use them in the wrong way. Lets share our feelings, can you feel me. Get real with the way you feel and deal with how you feel, let your guts spill if you want to live. Do not just lay back and chill because this is a big deal, stuffing your feeling is a act that can kill, People can like the way you look, but they will respect the way you feel. Its many products out the for how you look, and many pills for how you feel, pain pills, happy pills, anti pill this and anti pill that. Feelings oh feeling, will you look at your feelings. Its nothing that tell us how god looks, but he sure want us to know how he feel' He fealt so much for us that he sent his son to save us. He sent arks and profits, fire and rain. Your looks he made out of dirt but he told you to not harden your heart, your feelings his real concern. Feel good.

NOT TODAY

Keep on knocking but you can't come in. Tell your cravings and agrees to keep on knocking but they can't come in. Tell them to come back tomorrow and try again. Today they can not come in. When we live in the moment then today is now and tomorrow never comes. so they can come back because they will not knock us off track. One day at a time, tell your defeats, your fears, your worries and all bad things to come back tomorrow, today nothing is happening. No good go away today and do not have a nice day. Today you will not get no prey, I will not be prey today. To day I did pray. I before e except after c, so you see I put an a in my pray because I and my I comes before your e, and you use e in your prey. You drugs and alcohol you prey and try to take peoples life away. We pray for a better life today. Yes I before e except after c. Life before death. Prayers goes up and we are not down with drugs. My a in pray stand for A.A. and Aman. Your e in prey stands for evil. I see you and you can not come in. Keep on knocking but you can't come in, come back tomorrow and try again. One day at a time and today we win. Today we stick with the winners. We seek progress not protection and our e stands for effort. I love me and I love you, today we are ok. Today we pray. It only takes two to make a meeting. Meeting makers make it. Strength comes in numbers and when we are prayed up we get strong. The hunted can become the hunters. War on drugs, and now you are under attack. Attack us and we fight back. Tomorrow you come back. Today go away, just say no way today.

CAPTURED

The closer I get to you, the more you make me see, by giving you all I got your love has captured me. Who do you see fit to trust your love with. This title can apply to God, and yourself as well as others. Get close to god and closer to your self and it in turn will allow more trusting loving relationship with others. Kids, partners and friends. Then life can be sweeter than before. The more they make you see what life is all about. By giving all you got, its surely more that you will receive. You may have been captured by the police, you may have been captured by addiction or greed and lust. But when love captures you, it makes life worth living. Its such a beautiful thing to be captured by love. Also to get close to god is so much peace in ones life. It is always good and bad, so when you got captured in the addiction web, its just as bad as getting cancer in life changing ways. but you can be a bigger part of the heeling and recovery. In recovery you do want to give all you got, knowing the more you give or put in the more you get out of it. Not 50/50 love but 100%. I do not want to be little cancer but addiction is a life threatening disease as well as any disease that's life threatening. and we do have to take responsibility for our recovery. but not the guilt that the blame of getting this disease. Like any other disease we did not want it and it can and do happen to any and all people. Rich, poor, black or white, eastern or western, it does not matter, if you are human you can get it. And be capture in a wed of destruction.

ROAD RUNNER

The road runner and the coyote has a Unique relationship, almost like a drunk and his wine, or a dope fien and his drugs. The road runner is the alcohol or drugs and the coyote is us. We chase the road runner getting bumps and bruises all the time, yet we continue the chase. We shoot canon balls of denial to only drop back on our own heads, yet the chase is still on. We run into dark tunnels to get ran over by the train of confusion. The next thing we know we are hanging over a cliff on a thin tree branch wondering how it got this bad. Help is on the way in the form of a police officer or family lift us up. We are on the edge and they order us to treatment and/or A.A. / N. A. The road runner comes your way again saying beep beep, meaning get out of the way, make way. We quickly forget the cliff, the train that hit us and even the canon, the chase is on again. We are off chasing the road runner and the drugs again. What will you do this time?, drop the big iron weight over the cliff and fall over your self? Why not take the first step and admit we are powerless over drugs and alcohol. Admit my friend against the road runner you will not win. BEEP BEEP SURRENDER. PLEASE DO NOT TIE THAT ROCKET ON YOUR BACK. OR MONKEY ON YOUR BACK. Picture this that bird is like bird flu to you. This is a road that leads to jail or death. When you see this road runner, run! Run from him not after him. step one admit powerless, admit there is no win in using drugs and drinking. Beep Beep <its no fun when the road runner have the gun >.

DIET

Drug addiction is like weight problems in some ways. After getting sober or after losing weight you must make a life style change and commit to that change. Now staying sober require building new people in your life. I know of a man that stayed sober by staying away from old aquaintance but doing a slip or relapse he went back to old friends. Had he built new friends he would of had more to fall back on. Life style change is what will keep you stronger and sober longer. Friends are stronger than enemies, old friends are enemies of the state, state of mind. Get rid of the old bad friends and get new good friends. Get rid of old bad habits and get new good habits. Getting sober is first but staying sober is a life long job. It gets easy to do once you built a team and work with them, no need to do it alone. Its choices we make, good or bad. Habits, good or bad. Friends, good or bad. Its still time for learning and time for living, so lets.

MILK AND HONEY

I wanted to parallel a milk and honey story to a addiction and recovery story. We all know what the land of milk and honey is. Every thing is all good, such as money is flowing if you want to view it that way. The milk and honey stage of our using, its all fun, lights and action. But when the milk spoil it will make you sick. ITS NO GOOD WHEN IT GETS LIKE THAT. Honey is good but when you have to stick your hand in a bee hive to get it < its time to let go. At this stage it can cost you your life. We may have had some good days using but when the sun go down that day is over, never to return. But a new day is coming. Get the A. A. milk and the N. A. honey!!!!!! Maples is the land of milk and St. Paul is the land of honey When it come to the land of recovery. Mn is the land of lakes, in the mini there is plenty, plenty of milk and honey. We are the little apple but many many apple. Is big better or is the more the merrier? Not only the land of milk and honey but the land of lakes. Water, the living water will have a value in the days soon to come. We can count our blessing in many ways like the many lakes and treatment outlets for addicts. Our stores that sell alcohol close early and close on Sundays. A day of rest yes and we still compete with the city that don't sleep. The disease part of addiction we seek to treat. At the gopher state round up we all meet. To see all those recovering alcoholics is a treat. A. A. and N. A. there is no compete, welcome to all meeting and have a seat. In the land of milk and honey, in the twin cities we do not accept defeat.

CHANGE

I heard a man say that he learned that he has the power to change. WE to can change. We do not have power over our alcohol or drugs but we do have the power to see things different. It does not have to be the same. We can change our minds, our attitudes, and the people we hang around. We can change the places we go and the things we do. We can change the way we talk to ourself, all these changes will change your life some. Its not about change in your pocket but change in your life. All these changes take place on the inside of us and form on the out side. When we change our thought pattern, we change our actions and our life. Change the ideal that we have to do things alone. PRAYER—Lord help me be open for change. <>

WHAT DOES IT TAKE?

The answer to this question depend on what battle you are fighting. To make dreams come true it takes determination, passion, hard work, desire and guts. But that's not enough to over come a alcohol or drug addiction problem. It takes all that and more, it takes among those things and more! It takes humility, self inventory and awareness that you can not do it alone. It takes a high power and will power. It takes honesty, openness and willingness. It takes giving and receiving love, it takes service. It takes striving for progress, not perfection. This can be the biggest most important battle of your life, and it gives you the hope of making dreams come true. Sobriety must come first and not be stored on the shelf. It do not have a good shelf life, its part of your life and live it one day at a time.

LIFE OR DEATH

Watching the news today here in mpls, its all about life and death. Two people killed today, not their choice to dye. Today a jury sentence a man in North Dakota to death. Not his choice to die, but he chose to kill another, and even that's up for debate. They say his mental illness left him unable to control his actions. Now life and death at times can be a choice. We sometimes chose to dye slow deaths when we continue to use drugs against all costs and causes. As some couples turn violent against the other, so goes your relationship with alcohol and drugs. The thing you love so much turns against you. Get help and get out free. We all need a restraining order against drugs and alcohol too. Sleeping and dealing with the enemy, alcohol is no thrill and drugs really kill. We have to see that things or people that are good to us at first may not be good for us later. Once we let things or people in our lives, we have to step back after a while, or after the honey moon stage and take a real good look. Taking inventory of our lives is a thing to do daily, weekly and yearly. Small ones daily, and somewhat bigger weekly and full fledge yearly. Check out your self, and then check out the people and bad habits in your life. Its your life do what you got to do for you.

FATHERS DAY

The father is suppose to be the spiritual leader of the house hold. So what that tell me, he is meant to lead your family though the spirit., not the hand. Guard your spirit, and trust it, also nourish it so you can nourish others. The spirit protects you as well as your family. That's why they say A.A. and other programs is a spiritual setting. Many steps talk of spirituality and a higher power. Follow and surrender to your spirit and connect with your spiritual father. Just as your kids look to you as a father, you should do so also. PRAYER FOR TODAY—HEAVEN FATHER LET YOUR SPIRIT GUILD ME. We have one father here on earth, but two grandfathers and even four great grand fathers. The point here is the farther we go back in our family tree, we would end up at the apple tree with Adam and eve. That apple tree that was in the center of the garden, the tree of life, the tree of the knowledge of good and evil. Our heavenly father wanted to protect us from evil, but since evil is now a part of our life we need to protect our spirit. When the snake said we would not surely die if we eat of the apple, that was a lie. With the knowledge of good and evil, when we eat bad apples are evil one, our spirit start to die. That's why right away Adam felt naked, spirit was now dying and shame came, shame of our beauty. Now one bad apple do not spoil the whole bunch and we need to eat good apples, apples of aspiration, apples of atonement, apples achievement. The tree of life was filled with knowledge of good and evil. God is the father of our father here on earth, god is our spiritual and heavenly father.

HONESTY

I seen a sign today that said < bush lie and people die >. Well we as recovering people we have a great need to lie and cover up things. But in this program of recovery we need to be honest. If you want to jare your recovery to knew levels then practice being honest. When we lie parts of us die. Lies cause you to die and truth lets you grow. They say the truth sets you free. If you are struggling in recovery the biggest thing you can do is stop telling small lies. If you are not growing then lies are stunting your growth. Be accountable, be truthful, be real, be honest, be a conqueror and more. Have the complicity to be honest. THE TRUTH WILL SET YOU FREE!!!!!! Do not lie and this is why, a lie slow down your growth spiritually speaking. Even a little white lie can cause a small piece of our spirits to die. I do not know about you but myself and some others as well feel a small tremble in our spirit when we lie, its sort of like a small chill or small little shake we feel jolt though our body. Maybe a small measure of guilt or shame pierce or spirit. Then the other side of the coin is when we are truthful our spirit score a point of pride and honor, our morals gain a bit of foundation to build on in being a up standing person again. Its like people ask which one of the commandments are the most important, love is always above. People want to know which one of the steps are most important. Its no other steps without taking the first step in any journey. But word for word, each and every word is important, as is truth and honesty for growth in recovery. Why lie and make your spirit cry and die. NO LIE NOW FLY.

MOUNTAIN OR MOLEHILL

In our past life we always hoped that the trouble we faced was a mole hill, but there were many mountains to face and get over. Now we are not looking down but looking up. We now feel better in life and positive about our future. Half full or half empty? We now can look at the mountain as we did as kids, we wanted to be king of the mountain, rather than seeing it as over whelming trouble. The hill made us big and kings and gave us a task to reach out to achieve. Our lives can go from living in the valleys to living on top of the mountain. Our mole hill is now our house on the hill. As we change and think different, our actions are different and our lives are different. We have been though the ups and down in our lives and we can face life on life terms, be it mole hill or mountain. Do you want to be in the valley high or on the mountain sober? When you are high the mountain is like a mountain of trouble, but when you are sober the mountain is a hill for us to climb and be king of. Life is so different when you are sober, rather than drug on alcohol or drugs. Now we can live on the mountain high on life, not the valley high on drugs, drinking our spirits to valley lows. Do not turn your mole hills into mountains of trouble. Its in your hands now, how high or how low will you go. Put down the pipe, let those drugs go so your spirit can soar.

BE STRONG

Find your weak spots and build them up. In this battle we fight being strong in the physical sense is to no avail. We must be strong in our recovery. You know as addicts we learn quick to medicate pain of feeling and emotions. We can not cope with stress and boredom. Craving is another weak spot, so how do we learn to be strong. Just as building muscle in a gym. Repeated work over and over, know your weakness and firm them up with ammo. Affirmations work great, and self talk. Repeat them over and over, so when you come up on a bad moment you can fire away. Talk your self though it. Say to your self is it worth the short thrill for the long consequence. That moves you to great choice mode. Affirmation!!!!!!!!!!!!!!!!!!!!!!!!!!!!!!!!!!! Prayer—Lord help me Build my inner strength. I had to learn to be strong in spirit, just as I had to learn to be strong in the streets I grew up in. Being strong in the flesh is simple and easy, get the gold, get the girl. What did scar face say, get the money first and every thing else follow. What you see is what you get, you see some thing you want you boy it, hey every one got a price, right? Wrong! You give what belongs to this world there's, pay your taxes, but the price on the other side is like a camel though the needle plus giving all away and follow the big J.

CHOICE'S APPLE OR ORANGE

We as people have a great power that we sometimes use against ourself. To be able to chose is a great power. We can chose good or bad, freedom or prison. You can be in prison to a negative attitude, or a sinful life style and/or a drug and alcohol. We can chose against those things in our life, we have the power to chose life or death. Its a choice to keep it simple or put in the work of a rocket scientist. Easy does it, is a slogan we use in A.A., its a phrase you can live by and no pain no gain too. Put your energy into things you love, people you love. Chose your fight, do not fight against the system. do not step over the steps, work the steps so they can work for you. PRAY to make the right choices in life. We know that in drug addiction we look to be people that are very foolish in some of the choices we make. I think that's why people that work in treatment centers that have been a drug user and/or drinker can reach other addicts when trying to break though to us. We chose to open up more to someone that have been in our shoes. Apple or oranges, shoes or pants, we even can get better help with those that's been in our shoes than those that's been in our pants. Some one that's been in our pants can be great supporters, but on the flip side someone that's been in our pants can be big time enablers or distractions to our recovery. At times in recovery our partners can get confused about our new life and where they now stand. Old resentments can come up are the wrongs you caused may not be forgiven unless you put more effort into living to right your wrongs to them. The shoe fits in recovery sponsorship.

Apples for Addicts and Alcoholics

Book II

James Page Jr.

FORWARD

This book has a mission and that's to plant seeds of confidence. I would hope those seeds grow into self control among other things. One person can make a difference in the world and that's a fact. This can only be done by that person having self control. The spirit can lead a person, a family, a church, a community, a nation and even the world to peace. When we build our spiritual strength we can become strong in self worth, confidence, faith and love. All of life evil sins can be take on and over come. This book focus on drugs and alcohol, but we can take on any and all addictions, evils and sins. Rise people for Gods sake. We deserve sobriety, peace and love as well as health and wealth. Its good to take on worthy missions bigger than ourself, nothing or no one is bigger than God. When God is with us, who/ what can stand in our way.

INTRODUCTION

This book has been in the long time making. My name is James Oscar Page Jr, I am a Addict / Alcoholic and I approve this message. The message is that we can over come addiction with self help and help of others. We will over come our self, spirit over flesh. This book will feed your spirit and your spirit will become as popeye over drugs and alcohol and the brutis life style. I have had all I can take and I am not taking no more, you will have it your way if you hear what I say, you do not need to see it but you must believe it, then you will achieve it. Going green, spinach words for your spirit gives you super soul power. First I need you to know what my apples stand for and then you can stand with me. These apples will be for upliftment in life. APPLES stand for—All People Progress/Over Life's Evil Sins!!!! That's why we say apples for addicts and alcoholics. We will progress if we will to do so. In recovery practice makes progress. You can make a difference in your life by practice. I have a desire to up lift people so I wish to start a movement that I need you to be a part of, each one of us do our part by spreading spinach words will be a big start. The movement is a vision of Apples For All. Again—Apples for All = All People Progress/Over Life's Evil Sins, Faith/In Our Rise, Almighty's Love Lasts. That's apples for all and its a worthy cause, and will help you to help your self as well as help others. As Faith comes fear goes, and the brutis life style we are stepping on their toes. We all have seasons in your life, let change be the reason for the season, life gets better when you weather proof, I can't stand the rain, the heat, the cold and storms get old, time to spring into action. Apples for all, that's my call. The things I have been though in life got me ready and I am set to go. Talk to your self, talk to your spiritual self, because in the beginning was the word. So let it be good words you feed your soul, as the saying goes food for thought. Each one teach one that life can be what we will it to be, set your spirit free and eat the good apples off the apple tree. Spiritually speaking, a good apple a day will keep the evil/bad things away. Stand for something are fall for anything, it is not in Gods plan for you to be the fallen Man/Woman, you are more than welcome to stand with this apples for all movement. As Jesus request for us to feed his sheep, read this and other self help books and eat spinach words for your spirit to grow on.

JANUARY

Although I walk though the valley of the shadow of death, I will fear no evil. This is a popular verse out of palms. I want to look at this word for word and relate it to recovery some what. The first word is although, I put it like this, although meaning even though, yet and still. although the odds are against us we still fight on. That's word # 1. Word # 2 is I. I meaning me myself and I. Not my mother not my father but me myself and I. When we are going though something and our family or friends help us or do it for us, we thank them and give them most of the credit. instead of ourself or god the credit. Its something you must go though your self and no one can bare the burden for you. That's the 2nd word, now for the 3rd word walk. Walk not run, we run from bad things. We try to avoid the problem rather than facing it. We run by drinking or over looking it, not dealing with it. Have you ever notice when it rain and we run though it we get more wetter than when we walk. Walking show patience and perseverance as well as acceptance, but not defeat. That's the 3rd word and on with the 4th word. Though, though shows effort and success, not laying down are running. Once you go though it you own it and it possess no power over you. Also when you go though something it reveals your spirit to you, how strong you are. Stronger is he that's in you than he that's in the world. That's #3 and this is # 4 valley. The valley is the low point between the mountains, its also like our botten. You can learn more about yourself in the valley. You can receive more self strength in the valley of life. Do not get comfortable in the valley and dwell there.

Remember the other word though, walk though, do not stay in the valley. I hope you never fear those mountains in the distance never settle for the path of least resistance. That's the valley of and # 4. Now the shadow # 5. What's a shadow? Its a reflection, the only way to make a shadow is for darkness to get intwindle with light. So just don't see a dark shadow and think that's your lot, there is light somewhere near. You can not out run your shadow. Have you ever tried to stomp it away, or hide from it? Have your shadow ever scared you? Have you ever walked into a room and jump thinking someone was behind you, to only find your shadow. The only way to get rid of a shadow is in darkness or put light on it. Putting darkness on it would be isolation or drugging it away or negativity. The light on it is to expose it with truth. The light is the way and now for the next word. Word # 6 is of death. Its only a shadow of death. Since you are walking though this valley of the shadow of death, the valley is the low point, the shadow is darkness meeting light. If you are walking then you are not dying a physical death, so its that you or near a spiritual death. Low in spirit, low in self esteem and self worth. recall me myself and I. We need some light on this shadow of dark spiritual death. As long as there is a spark of light, then your spirit can come shining though. keep walking out of this dark valley and let your spirit guild you. Do not keep the shadow on with drugs or self pity or low self worth. Keep walking its much light on top of the mountain. You can reach toward heaven there where your spirit soar. Now # 7, I again. Its me oh lord standing in the need of prayer, me myself and I.

The next word # 8 is will. We all have a will, GOD also has a will for us. When we say I will, that means action, it means commitment. I will, not my will. I will over come, yes I will. Next word # 9 fear. Fear is opposite of faith, Faith heals and fear kills. God said he did not give us a spirit of fear, but of peace and joy. If GOD did not give us a spirit of fear, then where did that deadly spirit come from? It has to come from the evil one who come to steal, kill and destroy. Jesus told his disciples to fear not. He told them to take heart which means have faith, trust and believe. The bible say the only good fear is the fear of god. Wisdom is the fear of god and to shun evil is understanding. Evil is the last word. The bible speaks of the evil one. I believe some good people wrestle with a evil spirit that can be fought with the armor of god. I will fear no evil. Since I will means action, then I will not fear but I will fight evil. I will fight the good fight. When we fight we need to know our enemy, Ephesians 6 / 10-18 tells us who our enemy is and what we need to fight it. If we use the armor of GOD, we can not lose with the stuff we use. This is a spiritual fight and not a fight against flesh and blood. Our flesh is a tool used against us. We have to learn to feed our spirit more so than the flesh. Give the flesh what it needs, not what it wants. Give the spirit what it wants and needs, it wants life for us and wants it more abundant. Its needs love, I need love, the world needs love and love comes from above. Simon, peter and james. Have you ever heard that game Simon said? Not Simon cowl, But james said war comes from members of our flesh wanting.

God said a friend of this world is no friend of his. Which world do he want you to be a friend of? The street world, the material world of $ and more $ world opposite of the spiritual world. A. A. tells us their program is a spiritual program also. The recovery world takes very different views on life than the money, drinking and fast cars and movies stars. Its more so about giving rather than taking. Its about building people up rather than breaking them down. Telling the truth rather than lying, respect of others and the golden rule as a life tool. When we die a spiritual death there is nothing to fear, because faith that we have lived in line that our life style has likely gotten our name in the book of life, so death can not touch us. The 12 steps and the bible give us the same road map to living life in so many ways, the good book say your desire to tell the good news be like shoes on your feet. That comes out of Ephesians, where they talk about the armor of god. The 12 steps say carry the message. The message they want us to carry is of hope and the other bless the 12 steps offer us in the program. The good book say let the truth be like a belt around your waist. The 12 steps say we need to be honest. When using we walked though death pits all the time, back room dope deals and crossing state line for wine. Yes we walked though the valley of the shadow of death, now there is no fear of death here. We are to busy living to fear and worry about dying and we are word up with the sword, shields and all. Plus the team we roll with are not off bloody marys but they are bloody ready to do service work. I am walking in the rain with the one I love and it feels so fine, word up.

FEBRUARY PART # 1

IN RECOVERY STOPPING DRINKING AND DRUG USING IS ONLY THE FIRST STEP. To stop using drugs and drinking is not a easy thing, but once we stop we are on our way to getting our life back under control. Change is not easy to do in life matters. Changing who you are is next to impossible. But you can change the part of you that the world see and that your life is controlled by. You do not have to be lead by your flesh, Let your spirit be your guide. This will surely change your life in the 99.9 % range in my humble opinion. As I have said repeatedly in this well wishing book That if you live more in the spiritual realm of life and is lead by your spirit rather than the flesh, you will surely taste success. As god said a friend of this world is no friend of his, let me tell you that if you are a friend of the most high, you will be high on life. You will be a winner, and your concern for your life will not be hefty. You will likely think of others more than self and you will likely do much feeding of gods' sheep. I have heard that song in church, < yes Jesus love me, yes Jesus love me>. But do you love Jesus? Jesus told his disciples that if they love him then feed his sheep. When we are being guide by our spirit we think less of self and our own problems and think of others more. Also in A. A. / N. A. when we do service work and carry the message, is that not like feeding the sheep? Now I know I make this sound to easy and easy it is not. The flesh needs and desires are super powerful. Just as the urges to use drugs are too very very strong. We can not do it alone, we need higher power, groups of supporters and a program to follow. and more

SEE THOUGH

ONE OF THE GOALS WE INTEND TO REACH AT IN THIS BOOK IS TO SEE YOU THOUGH THE STRUGLE OF TURNING YOUR LIFE AROUND. We know we can not see though you to determine what we need to do to cure you. So since we know we can not see though you, can we help you to see your recovery though to the other side. The service I do help me, any thing I do to help others, in turn I am helping my self. I am a addict and I approve this message. This is a selfish program and new way of life I am living, but its not all about me. I take a knee so we can claim victory, I take two knees so I can claim my relationship with my higher power, my higher power is god. I was taught that one can not do it alone and need to fellowship. On the spiritual side one must not be selfish and help others when we can. On the personal side one must be selfish and personal take care of my needs and put no one or nothing before my needs or my program. What we put in we get out of recovery growth. We have to use the people that can hold us accountable to our self to rise above and out of the sick way of living. Denial and lying to our self and others is dead now, if we need a therapist or what ever it takes to keep it real with self. No more being so called true to the game and real or hard core down on the paper chase, but plastic to our spirit and inner morals. NO NO NO, its the other way around and its been backwards to being real in life that's more abundant to self and family that's really going to be there in the end. Though thick or thin, The body can be hard and thick, and the spirit can be thin and locked with in. Let it out.

FEB # 3 HOPE IS YOUR CHOICE

Power, control, choice, thoughts, action and the human will is all in our reach. Mind is the difference of success and failure and man is able to have choice over what we feed in or weed out of our mind. In your mind you can accept your lot or disregard it and realize the one you see fit for you. Mind is such a powerful tool, that once it is set with passion on a decision we are likely to realize it some way some how. Even on your dying bed, the body could be overcome with a life taking disease, but the mind still with will power decide when the lights go out. The mind can chose at times to fight on or let go. They have a thing that's called brain washed, where circumstances have power over ones mind. We have to give in to circumstances in order to have this happen. Because we are the only one that can order our mind to receive and believe a command. That's where we call others weak minded at times when they do things we can not picture and understand. But even in head injuries the mind is so tender and faguail that it can cost you your life easy. I know of a few people that bump their head and their life was never the same until their life was gone and the mind likely played a part in checking out. I think at times being smart is good but keeping your mind in check is key to success. We have to keep positive in and negative out of our mind. We have that power but as anything else its work and practice involved. Really no one but you have control over your mind, there are many many influences and temptation that can make it seen you are powerless. As anything else you can exercise for more mind control.

FEB # 4 MORE & MORE

   More and more we learn of mind power. Like a computer is related to a mind. How powerful is a computer, they about run the world for us. Every thing now is plugged into computer, from cameras to stop lights. Home business and all sorts of other deals. The real message here from me to you is the mind can do what you will it to do. And you need to practice mind self control. We can exercise to strengthen our mind to work with us. The mind can not keep you sober alone But it can send messages like you need to have help, you need to have a program. Other wise the mind will think it can do it on its own, and then to change your mind will be very hard. In the program of recovery the mind can be a enemy because its power to rationize and interlecturise. Those are some things that keep us in recovery from total submitting as step one require. This self help readings surely do work, I read so many of them myself for up lifting encouragement. I read < AS A MAN THINKET > by James Allen, its like a second bible to me. You can build yourself up by reading books like mines or the other james. His book is old but hold very true today now. He tell you that you are the master of your mind and the lord of your thoughts. I have read his book no less than 10 times, Each time I learn something new that stick with me. In recovery the mind is a tool that must be kept in check, distorted thinking, rationalizing, are overwhelming road blocks. The spiritual world have more simple ways of dealing with problems and they tend to be better in success rating. Mind over matter, make up your mind what matters. use or lose mind

THROW BACK

When I was using I fell in with a group of very negative people. I got to know them sort of like a few at a time. They all new each other for years and they all moved to the twin cities and bought their old city ways with them. I got to know one first and though him I meet the rest. They were not who I thought they were. Many times in the using life its a while before the true characters come to light. We need to know that the company we keep will surely affect us. Some of them are like fish you need to throw back. Just because it come out of the water does not mean its a fish. It could be a snake are a crab. That's not good company to keep, you know how crabs are in a barrel and how snakes are around a apple tree. The apple tree is the tree of life, we do not need to keep company with any snakes that's deadly to our spirit. Nor crabs that are jealous and lost and want to hold you back, throw them back. Its good for your recovery to watch the people in your life and throw back the ones that are negative. Some know what they know and that's all they know, with no room to grow. They do not even know when you step on their toe because they are so stuck in a one life trance that they think a little is a lot. Know need to put them down but get away from them and pray some day they will see another way. I would talk to a few of them about plans to lift our self in business, one would declare I could not do it. He believe he could not so he tried to place his low self courage on me. Then he would try to convince me to go the route of dealing ways because that's the standard of his self comfort and belief he could succeed at. That's a throw back and get away from. When I was using I would go around them but even a day sober I would stay away from them. Do not waste your time and dreams on those that's blind, petty and stuck in a one mind frame with low to no self worth and belief.

How do we get stuck messing with people we know mean us no good? Its only when we are not honoring our morals and our level of self worth that we are around people that's not on your level. I did it knowing these people did not have my best interest in hand. they were out to use me and I allowed it to a certain astint. They are so called friends and you can not trust them as far as you can see them. Yet you continue to go around them. You know the petty things they call their self getting over on is nothing to you, but your life and self worth is going down hill by being around takers and dividers in stead of adders and multiplyers. Then on top of that they are low in class, in game, in intelligence and self-worth. How on earth can you win around a bunch of losers, when you are in the boat with them trying to plan plot and stratize together. You are headed for a down hill crash, moral bankruptcy and/or a bit behind bars. The importance in the company we keep, the places we spend our time and the things we do are all going to determine how our life gets on or off track. Win or lose, stick with the winners and throw back the losers in your life now and for good. That can and will make all the difference in the world for your recovery. Not to put others down or your self up but you must be watchful and pickly as hell to not go though hell. Judge not a person by their looks and belongings because that's shallow, god judge hearts and tell us to test the spirits. We can feel and see a evil spirit most times. Dogs at times can see because it much animal abuse too. They too as we are looking for love. Do not look for love in the wrong places. Some you have to throw back, and sometimes you have to cast your nets deep. Some times you have to rock the boat and cast on the other side of the boat. Walk on the other side of the fence or wall. Will I kill so gods will live, mines is his and his is mines and his is best that need no test, throw back the rest. Watch the company you keep, the devil is roaming like a roaring lion seeing whom he can devour, chose gods power.

ONLY GOD KNOWS

Writing this book in the barber shop allow me to hear many many life stories. Both good and bad stories. It all reminds me that god gave us life and he is the only one that know for sure the out come and the end too. The resent story is of a family that put their love one on life support until all the family could get there to view him and pay their last respects. Soon they would have to pull the plug and let go and let god have his last say as god always does. The reason I title this only god knows is that this person was pledged with other disease that the doctors assumed would take his life, but this cancer came in strong and out of no where and invaded his body to take his life. The family was with this man two weeks earlier and all seemed fine, then two weeks later he is on his death bed without any power to walk. Only God knows when and how you will die. The doctors are experts on diagnoses but humans make mistakes, which leads to this relation, god does not make mistakes. You are not a mistake and god never gives us more than we can take. Pain is for a purpose and we all have a purpose too, so bear the pain and have no shame, also bear witness and shame the devil. Honor god and give him the glory, Jesus say have no worries. Since god got the world in his hands, we will call him the good hands man. Even though he is no man, he made man and made his son a man, he had a plan. God made a man with a plan and with a purpose because we are worth it, which makes god worthy of worship. I know I do not have all the answers as this is title only god knows. I do know that god knows! choice, chose god and win friend.

SUICIDE, FLESH OR SPIRIT

The pen is mightier than the sword, right or wrong? This can go both ways and it could be a trick question also. When the sword is the word of God then there is no right in that fight because we all know Gods might. But in street life when you live by the sword then you die by the sword, then the pen can be your friend. But check cashers and forgery people that thought they were slick in the game came up with this name game, they thought their way of robbing with the pen was better than robbing with a sword or gun. Then they end up in the pen and they need a pen pal and they need a sword or knife to protect their life. Do not get me wrong I do not put street people or any people down, I am they and by the grace of God there goes I. It's time for change, change from the sword to the pen, change your underwear, change the people we spend time with. Change the places we spend time at, change the things we do with our time. Change our attitude, our outlook and change our minds. Suicide is about killing of ourself. Why would we want to kill ourself? We are unhappy with self or the pain we feel become to much to bare. This is my opinion only and I tread light when I talk about suicide because by no means do I want anyone to harm themselves. My goal is to help you uplift yourself and live life more abundant in the spiritual sense. The bible tells us that our fight is not against flesh and blood. More or less its against the mind. Our mind is like a mine, we need to dig deep for minerals that's of great value. These minerals must first be put though the fire and pressure to transform them to shining diamonds or steel. You are no nut, you are a diamond in the rough. With support you can shine, it's your time. This I need you to hear and hear it clear, the suicide I want for us is the killing of self will, selfish parts of our soul. No part of the body at all do I want you to kill. I do want the desires of the flesh to be under control, do not over eat, do not just have sex with any one or for the wrong reasons. Self control is a wish I have for all and a prayer I pray for all. When you have self control, you do not think with your head at all, not big or little, you think with you heart and soul, but you must not be selfish when doing so, you must be in control of self and have self worth when deciding the things you want and need. Just as its good apples and bad apples, its good suicide and bad suicide, we must know the tricks of the evil one. the devil, on the apple tree is the knowledge of good and evil. Some good people can have evil actions, they can be blind to their evil deeds. They began to follow man and not God so much. To follow God half the time and man half the time, you or more valuable to the material world than to the spiritual world. To be a friend of one, is to be a enemy of the other. The devil will take you any way he can get you, but God do not take kind to part time. You can not be neutral because both worlds seek you, even when you pass away the seeking is finale and its no half and half, its one or the other then. Its more or less at this point that you made your bed that you will lay in. That's why I say kill your will, because the evil one is so slick and know how to play to the weakness and desires of your will and flesh. He tried the fisher of men, showed him the world he ruled, and offered it to him to bow down to him. The truth and the way said no way, he would not let his light shine in the devil darkness. The devil rule one world and tried to offer it to he that is in line to inherit the other world. The temptation that the flesh must face is out of this world. If you do not know who you are, you will fall for anything, rather than waiting on the something you are able to be a inheritance of as well. Staying in control of self, taking inventory and fellowshipping with spiritual people will keep you on the yellow brick road, not the blood slick road. Staying ready for the roaming devil and staying armored up with your shield and sword will keep you on the right road. On the wrong road is a load to carry and many friends you will bury. Do not carry that load, carry the message, be a living testimony, and for the love of Jesus, feed his sheep, good apples alone with hope, but surely no dope, no alcohol or bad spirits.

SUICIDE, RIGHT OR WRONG

The good the bad and the ugly, the horrors of life and the ability to cope, we have to get it out of our mind that we need dope, to change this out of our mind and mine into energy for life to be lived more abundant. Suicide, not flesh and blood but the evil in the realm of the mind. The weapon we use for this fight, the armor of God is the weapon we should chose. Now one way suicide is a sin is what they teach us, and the word of God also say we must kill ourself to get closer to him. Die to live, and James say that war comes from the flesh wanting to feed their filthy needs. Although our fight is not against flesh and blood, we must kill the desires of the flesh. To succeed in our quest for holy aspirations the flesh must be tamed and chained, the spirit must be fed and freed. What do James say is hard to tame, the tongue for the words they speak, I say also the pen for the words they write. Word against word, so we need the sword against the pen of flesh writing. A double edge sword for the pen and the tongue, come out swinging both ways. But life can not be lived in peace both ways, make up your mind which master will you serve, flesh or spirit. Mind over matter, it's a matter of mining your mind and digging deep in self inventory. They tell us we cannot serve two masters, also money makes a great servant but a poor master. Dig deep and get to the root, is money the root of evil. Two wrongs don't make a right, which enemy will you fight. Flesh and blood or the spirit of love, eat fruits of the spirit so you can feed your spirit and starve the flesh. Evil you can not will it away, you have to kill it away, the right way, the godly way, take your shield in this war we need to kill our will and then Gods will live and the spirit will be filled. Holy aspiration rise.

KILL WILL, SUICIDE

When the spirit rise, the flesh go low down into the dirt it knows its place back to where it came from. What's in a name, when there were slaves the master give them their names. God told Adam to name names. When Adam saw Eve he said WO man, that's woman, bone of my bone and flesh of my flesh. The spirit comes from God and only God. The short name for Willie is Will. Free Willie because serving our will can be a whale of trouble, making us want to commit suicide. The spirit of Willie Lynch when dealing with humans he consider to be slaves was evil. Willie we will lynch the evil spirit and free Gods will. Willie Lynch your will was to kill, steal and destroy and you was the devils toy. We will lynch Willie and kill our will, we will free the whale Willie, but not the Willie will that's a whale of misery to our spirits. We choose Gods will to live in us and for us, not the will of Willie that wants to kill us and divide us. As Gods people united we stand and divide we fall. Stand for something or fall for anything. When mans spirit was low then came the fall of man, because the evil plan of a snake to divided us from God and fill our spirit with shame and guilt, not the love and peace god had given us. You know your life is low when you hide from God you have shame of something you have done wrong. Lay your burden on God and seek his forgiveness his mercy and grace. Willie taught slave owners to divide and conquer. To enslave people you must break their spirit. He wanted the slaves to not trust God or each other and have no faith. Rely on their masters for everything. We know man will let you down every time as will false gods also Willie Lynch

PRIDE SUICIDE KILL WILL

Even some so called masters are out serving false gods and they are enslaved to a evil spirit themselves. This is about drugs and alcohol attacking our spirits, but our spirits are so fragile and tender that even a small white lie causes part of our spirit to die. Our spirit needs hugs not drugs, love not hate, unity not division and faith not fear. Willie Lynch in his speech about how to control your slaves, brags of his success in being a master, but the whale of sacrifice he had to give up was the selling of his own soul, heart and spirit. To turn man against God is to sell your soul to the devil. Most people in those days at least wanted slaves to believe in their god and have faith there in. Lynch tried to divide and swindle the foreman, the slaves and all to the point of making the slave owners gods themselves. That's how he viewed himself in his bragging, at the level of God. Yes he was the devils toy and he believed in the worst of false gods, himself. To put yourself on the level of God is full blown denial or devilnial. That is how the devil got cast out, trying to compare and take the place of God. To attempt to be godly is a big enough task but to try to be God is a whale of a tale and a friend of the devils world. It was a big mission to free Willie and a great cause, lets be civil not evil. Lets fight for civil rights not evil wrongs. The devil can tell a whale of a tale and that's how man fell. The fallen man with Jesus hand we can stand again. Listen devil and Willie it's silly to think you are greater than God and hide behind a mask, down you will be cast and fast like trash. No divide, with God we belong and put no man on his thrown, Gods people united we stand. AMEN

USE IT OR LOSE IT

When you are given a gift, a talent or a skill, you need to use it or lose it. Practice makes perfect is a saying that's common. But I do not believe in perfect, but something can be so good that it's great or even 99.9 % that's near perfect. Point here is that use what you got or lose what you got. Also the point is that with practice you get better and you keep you skill well polished. To take anything for granted is not showing gratitude. Work is rewarded and hard work is surely rewarded. The right kind of work can help to make you happy and the wrong kind of work can cause misery in your life. If you are doing work you enjoy and getting paid for it then its a blessing in your life. You can apply yourself into it with passion and more than likely you are making a difference in someone's life, or bring in money to the company you are working for. Better yet you could be working for self, or a great cause. If these are God given gifts and we show gratitude and put in work that's a service to better others life and to glorify God and goodness as well, then rewards are stored up in more than just bank accounts, and joy is bouncing all over the place. If this gift is not accepted with gratitude and taken for granted or even used for selfish or evil reasons then instead of rewards there will be consequences to pay. Sometimes these consequences can be just losing the skill or talent, and other times bigger loses like freedom or even life itself. Practice and gratitude are habits that are usually rewarding, they are such huge tools to use in life and in recovery as well.

USE IT OR LOSE IT

When we use drugs it will be consequences regardless of the way we get out. If we get out with our life we should have gratitude for that as well and try to be a blessing to others once we make it through. Many do not make it. Some get clean and they later pay anyway, they find they have done damage to an organ or some other problem that we have to suffer through. The rich and famous too, Whitney was given a beautiful voice and a career to cherish and drugs came and done it's damage. It can happen in many ways to pay, loss of your voice, loss of respect and loss of the many great opportunities just do not come as easy. What will you be remembered for most? London reported a concert she had over there, where people walked out and some plugged their ears. For a moment I felt sorry for her, but she do not need that. She has been blessed with a gift and whatever God see fit for her is between he and she. She was at the top of her field and like Mary J a comeback is in their hands and the good hands man that have the whole world in his hands. There are lessons there for them and all to see. It's not what happen to you, but what happen in you that is more important in the come back and the outcome as well. How we deal with problems can be worse than the problem itself and the way we view it has a great amount of power in the effect. Are we grateful for the way we came out of this ordeal? It could always be worse and if we use it to Gods glory it can be a huge tool to reach people in need of spiritual upliftment.

It's not over until its over, it's not over until God says its over, God has the first and the last say each and every day. We can renew our strength when we plug into Gods charger that do charge us up good and do not charge us because his grace is freely given. When we give up our will and we go out of our way to serve Gods will, surely goodness and mercy shall follow us all the days of our life. Days of our life will become a platform to practice our gift and use our talent for a higher calling and a purpose in helping mankind live life more abundantly. Days of our life will take on new meaning for us and give us a chance to redeem ourself. Days of our life will give us a chance to be a role player in our loved ones lives, it's not over until its over. Days of our lives will become more sunny as we stand on top of the mountain soaring in the peace and serenity of Gods grace. Days of our lives will be days rather than nights of drug use and abuse and misery, shame and pain while darkness hunt us every waking moment. Days of our lives will afford us a chance for payback, a opportunity to give and give back, to be able to right some of our wrongs and to redeem ourself in the eyes of our loved ones. To be able to have some dignity and respect for ourself and see in our kids' eyes a proud look is a joy many people would love to have one more chance at. The things in life we miss and treasure most are simply all about feeling of others outlook on us. If we are given a chance to change something before we go, it would be in the relationship dealing of people, loved ones. Days of our life, use them or lose them, use the gifts God gave us.

Use your family's love or lose it, your girlfriend or boyfriends love or lose it. To take someones love for granted is an awful thing. Just as they say a mind is a terrible thing to waste. To waste a gift given you by God is a sad thing to face, face to face. It's a perfect way to learn your place and earn your place in this rat race where money we chase day to day. We can get lost in this big fast moving world and lose our way with all the temptations get caught up in drug use and drinking for stress management. To check out of our mind some time, pop pop wiz kid oh what a relief it is to get out of our mind. Our mind can be a scary place sober, confused, overwhelmed with pressure and expectations. The burden and the load we have to carry makes it hard to carry on, we must not give up or give in to the fast fix tricks that cost us more in the end. I know its hard to cope, the days of our lives we are hanging on the rope and life is pounding on us hard and fast, hitting us with everything. Rope or dope was one mans plan, but he had the most high in his corner. That's why he was able to fight for what he felt was right, at high costing prices. He had hope and faith and belief and the vision that he was a champ of many fights and causes. With God with him he felt he could not lose, and more important he was willing to lose to serve a higher calling. With faith and hope we can cope without the use of dope. We know that what dope offers is false and it has a hidden cost, using it too many lives have been lost. Ruining a family's chance at a peaceful unity and roots planted deep in truth, honor values and morals with our God.

SPEAK LIFE

Recovery is a all in decision, not a luke warm person that is sober today and drunk tomorrow. Sure a relapse is a part of the new way of life, and so is a slip. This new life of sobriety is about change and spiritual progress. No room for faking or luke warm player. I heard that a luke warm addict in recovery is a tool for the weak to use. We in recovery do not want the new comers around the luke warm addicts and the half in ones. This is not a 50/50 change and the other 50 hang onto old life ways. No this is in with the new and out with the old. New ways, you got to know when to hold them, old ones you got to know when to fold them. We are all in around here and those faking or not sure will not go far with us. We are like Adam the apple man, with eve we are all in, shake the snake, we are not like doubting Thomas, not show me state attitude this time, this way of life is tried and proven. We have faith in this new life style and blindly follow the ones that lead the way, all others move and get out the way. When the user move and use they lose just like that. Its not good that man be alone, if you are in recovery then you are bone of my bone and flesh of my flesh, but spirit is best, that I will share a part from my heart. Its a new day and a new way and today its ok and I am not going to play, I am going to stay. No luke warm, our power is higher and we are on fire. For getting high there is no desire, we get stronger by the hour. We are covered in a love shower, what drug use has to offer we do not want any more, we know the score. we do not want to return where we were before. No 50 / 50 its all in now.

WHO TOLD YOU THAT

So they say seeing is believing, I say words are for up building and life filling, now some use them for spirit killing. I want to help change that view if god is willing. Sticks and stones can break your bones but words can never hurt. I think some one used the statement of words will never hurt as a affirmation to fight against words hurting them. Words can kill or wound parts of your spirit and cause you to feel weak in your self worth. But on the same token words can build up your spirit so what someone else say to you and about you will not have the impact that they could or would on someone that's not worded up with affirmations. Self inner strength is important and the way to build one self up is to listen and talk with others on this subject, but self talk is very clear a self strength builder. On the Tyra Banks show she had the women on that bleach their skin because they did not feel comfortable or pretty in their own skin. I thought of god when he came looking for Adam and eve in the garden, and they hid from him. When he found them, they said we hid because we were naked. GOD SAID WHO TOLD YOU THAT. I say who told you your skin is ugly. I know god did not say so, when god made all men and women, he seen them and said that's good. God do not make mistakes. That's back to words, we have to word up in God's word. Seeing is believing. But we need to learn to see with our hearts eye. There are the minds eye, the heart eyes and the plain eyes. Even they say the eyes are the mirror to the soul. Feed your spirit good words, and love which is a fruit of the spirit. Apple is the first fruit, god is my first love, neighbors.

ROCK AROUND THE APPLE TREE

A apple a day keeps the craving away, daily reading apple style. a apple a day keeps the argues away in a spiritual way. A apple is no crime you can have mines. Apples for addicts and alcoholics. No longer give apples to the teachers, they can have oranges or plums because when it comes to this addiction thing they are dumb. They say will power, but drugs have kill power. Chemical dependency have disease power, craving and yearning come by the hour. We need a higher power, it can not be done on our will power. But a we around the apple tree can set us free, the apple tree stand for community. I do not have the answer, and there is no I in team. We all need to nourish and eat off this tree, the apples are free and will set us free. No fear of the snake to deceive us, its a lie if you think drugs will alieve us. No running and hiding from our higher power, his arms has always been open to receive us. The naked truth was meant to relieve us, now we are covered in guilt and shame, pointing fingers as if everyone else is to blame. Now in a toast we hold up a bloody mary to relieve us, but Mary's son blood came to retrieve us. You can act leery, you can get teary you need not live in feary, this program is based on spirit. I want this to be clear, no more denial, to lie is to die, I want to see you fly, but do not do it high. Step up one at a time, 12 steps will be just fine, an apple is no crime, you can have mine. N. A. and/or A. A. apple tree is in their prime. An apple is no crime always remember you can have mine, stop by a meeting and plenty apples you will find, one day at a time.

LIFE LEARNED LESSONS

Lessons in life are learned early on and they are learned settle too. What can you do but learn what you learn, and believe in your teachers and role models. This is no pity party but my role models were the wrong ones to nourish me and build me up with positive habits and morals. I have a huge family of three sisters and seven brothers. I love them so I can and did grow to follow their lead. The sorry thing is that their lead was none of us graduated high school to go on to college. At the age of fourteen I was visiting my brother in prison. Me, my mother and my brother that was sixteen at the time would drive up to visit my older brother in prison. He would tell my mother that if the guards did not see you getting visits, then they would think you had no one to care and they would do anything they please to you. He would have us to hold letters as proof that they had threaten him. This was my role model, I did my first crime with him, smoked my first weed and snort my first line of heroin with him. He gave me my first gun, and my other big brother was the one to shoot me up with a needle. He stole my first girl friend and told me he was showing me how they would do me out in the world. He messed my world up for sure, but it was on me to get it all together once I aged to make decisions on my own. I can not blame him or others for my personal growth and my recovery. Gods grace and will for you depends on none of that stuff. I had three younger than me so I had to take on a role of big bro for then with what little I knew in life myself. Life goes on and here we are today, me on a mission to get things right in my life.

In some life lessons and sayings, they say every thing happen for a reason. Once I put some faith in that saying and began to believe in gods will for my life, and started to have thanks for what I had, not pity about the bad breaks in life, I seen that choices are real and one can dream and seek it with passion, we stand to go against the odds. To be happy are successful in life it takes work. To accomplish goals toward money and business it takes belief and determination. Belief is a state of mind, and to be determined to achieve is when one goes after the goal. Also even the rich has to work at being happy, its also a state of mind that do not just happen by luck, one must make up their minds and make right choices, and go after it, and not be willing to let any one or anything take that away. Regardless of your past, or your circumstances, your state of mind and belief and thought pattern can effect what you gain out of life. Things in life will hinder you but its help out here and one must seek out the help and use it, apply it and help yourself and never give up. Another saying is god help those that help their self. No matter how bad it gets your life is in your hands, never give up, its to many things out here that's against you, so you do not need to be against your self too. Life will have its ups and downs, that's life, enjoy while the going is good, but be strong when times get hard. Saul became Paul, and Jesus named his disciples new names. Even when good boys go bad, you can have pretty tony turn to tuff tony, but in recovery you are now tony the tiger. Time to get it right in life now no matter what you been though.

When we learn in life these lessons can be used for good or bad. If you have had real life experience then we can take these and make good out of them. Many things we go though in life makes us strong and we need to find a need for those life strengths and apply them to help ourself and others, Take someone that has been counted out, you can make a great difference in many lives by showing you had what it took to turn things around. A testimony is proof, talk it and walk it and let it show, let your light shine to bring another out of the darkness. Do it for your self and watch how many lives you can affect, you do not know now how many lives you are affecting in bad times, the good times you will do twice the influence to other needy people. I had a strong revelation that the damage you do in life to yourself, your kids, your love ones and your community, can be made up for. What we do in life do not just effect our self, it will surly have meaning to others as well, good or bad. If you live in the modern world and are given the chance to have access to tools like this book, you are blessed with help near at your hands, We have the internet and riches and government help. Its always some one in worst standing when you look at it, you are blessed. But there can be many many hidden enemies in our lives, mental illness, negative influences in our lives. Kids can start in life with a under hand, mental ill parents, or they can have the disease of alcoholism, or just plain old bad role models in their life with little to no loving nourishment. Then the odds go down but there is still hope, so learn to cope.

I want you to know its no big I and little you in these self help reading I put out, I am not a know it all. Now after 600 months of life I do know a thing or two, and that's a thing or two I want to share with you. And to get you to look at your life and not make a life taking mistake, I will talk about drugs here a little. The main theme of this encouragement writing are to turn you from using drugs and drinking alcohol. That's only one corner of the issues I want us to take a look at. Mental illness and criminal life style living, the hustle and bustle of the game of life. Any unhealthy living and self defeating choices we make to be cool or to be one of the crowd. Also any choices we make thinking we have our life laid out for us and this is all there is and this is the way its always been. Months, I have been a live 600 months. If you are selling drugs as your life choice to survive then look at the time and term in months. A three time loser will get over 300 months, that's easy half my life time, and yea to much time for people that have choices. Once we stop looking for the easy way or the quick way, we will look at the best way. Do that there and see where your yellow brick road take you. You will get around that up and down crap. Enough of thinking we have to do what we can rather than what we want to do. Just do it and just say no to drugs, both using and selling them. Take this next point to heart. People blame failure on environment and circumstances. Both of those can be very true, that's in this world, but in the spiritual world there is no failure. That's why spiritual programs can take the worst of the worst and bring out their best of their best.

ONE IN A MILLION

One in a million chances of a lifetime. A million chances and still striding. Struggling and trying to get it right. God's way is right and my way is wrong. God is a god of a million chances, many many chances. If his spirit did not dwell we would not stand a chance in hell. God made us all unique and out of a million it's only one you, no one in the world is like you. Similar yes, but like you no. It's not the color of your skin, your size or looks that make you you, or make you different. Nothing you see makes you different, it's God inside of you, The spirit that comes from God that makes you you. God breath his spirit of life in us and blessed is the spirit of god. God is good and I did wonder how God had the whole world in his hands. The spirit world? Now I can see what he means by a friend of this world is not a friend of god. Two worlds, the physical and spiritual. One me was made out of dirt and dirt it will return to and the other me was made when he blew his breath of life and spirit into me. The body and the soul. The body goes down and the spirit goes up when we die. When we live out here the body crave sex and the spirit crave love. Love come from above or you can get down with dirty nasty sex. Dirt down, love me up. Even these saying tell us in so many ways the difference of the two worlds. We must put them in their place. Which one rules your life. Which one do you feed the most, which gets more of your time. Which do you recognize or most proud of? Which is stronger and rule your life? The body crave fun, the spirit crave joy and peace. The body wants to be seen and heard and feared. The spirit wants to be a help to the sick, the weak the underdog. The body want to rub shoulders with the rich and famous, the spirit wants to be among the sick in hospitals, jails and homeless shelters. One you and one God, take your million and use it well. The body wants to be in nightclubs partying with the girls or guys, the spirit wants to visit the needy. Chose life or death, it's time to live the real life that means peace on earth to all and self.

WHAT DO IT TAKE FOR YOU

What do it take for you to make your life major change? Do you have to see it done, some say seeing is believing. Some learn by bumping their heads over and over again. Some it takes all those things and more, I fit in the hard core area of change. I put my life on the line so many times before I would make that change. Then we have to prepare our self after we make the needed change to align our self up to hold on to the new life we have gained. We do this by figuring out how and why we got caught in this web of destruction in the first place. We do not do this to blame others or have a self pity party, we do it for change and for life, and a purpose. We get strong to help others alone the way. We can not go back and make up for the things in life we did wrong but we have to not make the same mistakes, nor teach others self defeating habits. When we learn the best us we can be, then we can be a role model for some one in life. People grew up watching my bad habits and want to be like me, so I have to take the blame that I was not a good model for a needed person in life. The same thing happen to me, but I have a chance to turn that around by turning my life around and do some major good out here and give back to the community. Take on a purpose with passion, and instead of being a dope fien, be dope when dealing with the needy and the young. No more dope dealing and dope using but, dealing with the users and getting them a fix on faith and feeling that can alter their life, that they can be moral supporters of their young. Time to turn this all around and help one person as well as myself change.

HARD TO CHANGE

In some of these mini stories I write, I do them out of a barber shop owned by a great woman and dear friend. As I spend days in the shop I get to see and hear all sorts of people as they come and go. The shop cut many arm forces men, do to the fact she work on the base before opening here. Being that she is a great hair cutter, a woman and a very likeable person many people followed her over here. Some of the issues they go though is like those of addicts and those of people in recovery. Its called life happening. One big deal is change, it happens and it at times need to happen. Some of the guys come back home and their role has been filled in the family. Other times these guys go over there the routine is clear cut. they can lean on others for support of having your back in life threaten ways. But who to lean on about feelings issues, they all learn to be hard men and fight, not cry about your girl moving on, who then can you lean on. Come back home to a home hero welcoming but you are now hooked on drugs and drink to not think. Life has went on without you and you need help putting your life back together. The wife been carrying the load with the kids, now you also with your mental illness issues. What do you do with your life now, unlike over there when you knew every minute what to do. Yes as a addict needs change and support and understanding thus does all people with problems. United we stand and divided we fall. Over there all for one and one for all. We need to respect all and no big me and little you attitude. As driving on the road, we need to see motor bikes, we need to also stop seeing crying as soft. Its much to cry about but we need to see with our inner eye and cry out of our heart where it hurt. It will take change to make things work.

MY SHARE

Once you get a goal and set out to get it, let nothing or no one get in your way. Get out of your circle and think out side of the box. Not do just addicts and alcoholics have issues that disable us in life, but men and women getting out of the arm services and people dealing with tough life issues as well are having their problems. What can we do, we have to look at the problem from other perspectives. I am not a know it all, nor do I have the answer for your problem directly. A common answer toward problems is to view them with open ears, eyes and mind. Be willing to try it new ways. That's where greatness come in at, change and willing to accept help from unlikely source with out pride holding you down. Do not mix pleasure and business. Also listen to the wise people that came before us and their knowledge that they grew though. One is do not lend family and friends money. They learned these wise things and passed them down to us so we would not have to repeat their mistakes. Listen and apply wise advice to our lives is being wise ourself. Get smart by getting humble, to be a great leader we have to know how to be good listeners and able to apply ourself to what we know that's proven to work. If the faith of a mustard seed can move mountains, our only hurdle to conquer is ourself. Get down on yourself without getting down on yourself. Self made, self worth, self motivated and self control. Conceive, believe and achieve. Be centered and not self centered, get to rely on inner feeling and strength to be independent. Devoted and determent to succeed attaining self-reliant power. With god what can we not do when we go for it.

TEENS NEED SAFETY

Teens like to have parties and its part of learning to communicate in life. Today's teens have many many things to be aware of. This writing come from the deadly week on our roads in mn and the amount of teens in these crashes. For life to begin and end so fast is a rude awaking for people in our state. It has people taking a serous look at teens and their driving privileges. Should they or should they not be able to drive at this age. Also we have to take a look at alcohol in these deadly incidents. We have to look at the rules, the parents and all factors that we can view in a attempt to protect our young people and all the people that share our roads. Minneasota is a leader in treatment for alcoholism and drug addiction, and that makes addicts proud. Many people came to this state to go to treatment and get their life together, they stayed and got into the field of helping others. Some of the teens in the car crash this past week had just gotten a presentation on safety before they lost their life in circumstances we desire to get a better grip on. We will get better control, but there is text message, drinking and driving among phones, make up and radios to take their attention off the road. We will keep trying to get though to them. We have great men like Mark Dayton that has went though this and is not afraid to take a stand on the horrors of alcoholism and its reach to all people. Young, old, black or white and the rich and poor as well. We are all affected by the safety of our roads, the disease of alcoholism and drug use. Life in Minnesota will be left to the young to carry on and we want to keep a grip on the horrors of drinking for all and double for teens new drivers. Big O has made a huge impact in the lives of many, but I want to personal thank her for the phone message campaign while driving or riding in cars.

H, H AND H / HELPING HAND AND HEART

When the young get their start they make many proud in their heart, you want to give them a hand to show just where you stand. From little girl to lovely lady, from a bouncing boy to a self made man, its time for us to cheer from the stands. All their friends are on the side lines and we raised them right so they will be just fine, we are always at the reach of a dime. We have to let them go and let them fly, let them try, but do not let them die. What can we do to get a hand on the problem here, we can not live our life in fear, they are in our hearts dear and near. We have to make the rules very clear, and with tough love we have to enforce these rules, so no bad news are life long dues, just follow and enforce the rules. We have to go to any measure because these are our treasures, to see them grow is our pleasure. We want our kids to have fun, but to lose your life it do not only take a gun, its to many ways under the sun. So follow the rules cause we love you, golden rules, safety tools, our hearts will melt, just buckle your belt. Keep on driving and keep on thriving, the sun is rising, with its golden shining, Follow the rules, because we love you, use safety tools, and the golden rules, our hearts will melt, so buckle your belt. Now keep on driving and keep on thriving. Mind over matter, you matter and you are mines. One more time. BUCKLE YOUR BELTS AND SAFETY RULES PROMISE TO USE. This is written by james and sue, from crosstown to you. Crosstown the helping hands and hearts barbershop. CROSSTOWN BARBERS In buckled seats you have a better chance of surviving a crash.

MY SPACE

Sharing this world with other people we have a responsibility to respect over all rules to not risk the safety of others. This mini story comes from the news in mpls on 4-25-10 of all the deadly crashes on our roads today. Today they have not confirmed if alcohol played a part this time or not. We do know that most of the deaths were teenagers and one of the drivers had their license for only two weeks. That driver broke a few rules by driving after midnight and also having to many others in the car under age I think. But one man that teach driver safety came on the news and said that the parents have to sign for them to be able to drive. In signing they are taking responsibility for their kids. We all have to be more responsible and aware of the need to follow rules and practice safety. To have the privilege to drive is almost like a right of passage, To hear youngsters talk about when they got their driver license you understand the importance of this new level in life. I heard two kids talk and they talked about how old they were when they got their license. One at 16 and the other at 19, it was viewed almost as a sin by the one 16 that the other would wait so long. Its certain things that at this tender age these kids think is a must. Sex, drinking at a party among other things, and the parents do not get to sign off on these. On all these things we take space on we can communicate with our kids, and talk about the risks and the responsibility and the need for safety. Some things in our space on this earth is a right and others are a privilege, we need to honor those and value our life as well as others. Life is fragile so cherish yours.

YOUNG MAN THOUGHTS, DUMB MAN THOUGHTS

Things are crazy, I'm not lazy. I do not know where I fit in, I have not made my life plan to get in. Forty years old and life is cold, I use to be conceded and bold. All the world I felt I owned. I did not have riches to claim that made me feel I own the world, many people had far more as far as material things go. I had pride and I had a spirit as hard as iron. Life I thought was all about me, no one could touch me as far as I could see. When it came to some things I could care less, and with most things I thought I was the best. Being young had lots to do with it. But life is a gift that learning will come regardless of yearning or earning. Life will stand you up and sit you down. The game of life you will play and it comes a day that you will lay. Sometimes you will not listen to what anyone has to say. Then it will come a day when you will tell God to have it his way. It's funny how we do not have a clue but we go though life thinking its all about you. Get lost lose yourself, it's one of the best feelings I ever felt. Drinking and ghetto thinking make street foes turn to finking. Every dog has his day, every player wants to play. Every man on trial wants to hear nay. I want to be in the mold of the potter's clay. Not on my own but it's hard to know that when you feel alone, every dog wants a bone, every child needs a home. Every man have the desire to belong. It's a small world, togetherness best explained like boy meets girl. The things you think and feel when you are young, will be rejected as dumb when most of your life is done. Live and grow wise and look at life with new eyes. Know that time flies, so no more lies.

THE GAME OF LIFE

Life is not a game! Addiction is not a game either. For the sake of life we are about to look at addiction as a game of football. This game can either save your life or take your life. Lets say in addiction you are on the offensive team. They want to score drugs or points. We are after scoring fun, good feelings or pain killing. We run short plays, sneak plays and always trying to score. If we can't get a touchdown we settle for a field goal. If we can't get heroin we settle for oxycontin pain pills. If we can't get a glass pipe we settle for a can. Can't get a blunt we settle for a joint. Soon we can't even get a first down and we get many penalties and fines. It is now 4th down and time is running out and its another losing season. You get injured and traded and no one trusts you or wants you. You go to jail and teammates forget you, But the team of N. A. or A.A. picks you up, they lift you up. Now you are on the defensive team. No scoring is what we fight for. Keep drugs and alcohol out of our end zones and homes. On this side of the ball is a different life. No passing drugs around we block passes now. Offense wins some games, but defense wins super bowls. You can be champ with a key ring and on a super bowl team. The grass is greener on this side of the ball, just ask the Williams wall. Now that you have a new life that you are carving do not kick that ball to Percy Harvin. Bret Farve play though the pain, having sobriety is not the same, living a sober life you have much to gain. Cravings and urges at times can be like a hunger monster, do not feed it, not even rice, that mans hands ain't nothing nice. I know your spirit can be scared, the disease of addiction will not keep running over us, we have jarred. We are out to win and we do not play, we have E. J. so you can keep your e and j. Now we know for sure that life is no game and life will throw things your, we have to play the hand we are given. Alcoholism is a disease that is addictive, and when it comes to fighting drug and alcohol addiction we are all on the same team. Team USA united we can win, N. F. L. & N.

H. L. & N. B. A. & W. B. A. and Base Ball we all will join in the fight to get it right. Soul searching and sober living, life is a one time thing so we face any and all trouble life can bring. We have to live and take the good times and the bad, but drugs will take away the good times we once had. We know life is up and down but alcohol is a downer that we do not want around. Just as cigarettes can give you cancer, alcohol and drugs can give you the disease of addiction. Addiction disease just as cancer can shorten your life and cause all kinds of misery too. The vikings are a great model, four super bowls and no ring, but they keep playing as a team and chasing the dream. Not a quilter but a go getter, no one is a loser until they give up, we too must not give up but get up. The only thing we are going to give up on is the life of using drugs as a crutch and the using and the bozzing. Part of living life is to take what life is giving, do not be mating with the ones that's hating, do not try to go through life by skating, get up and walk and carry your cross. You think that drugs make you better at dating until your values start fading. The big thing I have learned in life is feed your spirit, protect your heart, and other things is little things. Be a good team player is better than being a good player. Addiction is a disease, say cheeze and get that picture please. REAL TALK < NO GAMES by JAMES > Get on the winning team of N. A. hey.

CRAVINGS

Some people thought that it was nothing more intense than the lustful desire for sex, or hunger pains. Also the thirst for water. But they don't know what an addict in early recovery goes through. When something triggers that craving, it can be so very intense. It can send you into denial very quickly, walking out of a meeting or even a long term treatment center. The desire can come anytime, in your sleep or dream or even in church. But the other triggers like people, places and things can really trigger a craving. These cravings can be so powerful for a short period that we think its useless at times. They will pass. But we need the tools to make it through this strong desire short period. In early recovery the slips and relapses from cravings cause many to fall quick. We are easy to see the good times in our past using life but we need to always be able to recall the trouble times. We do not need to see them for the reason of a pity party but the seasons of the storms and cold cold days. The mind can trick us if we do not play the tape all the way though. There was some good times in using but when you eat the fat, you do not just get the flavor you get the calories also. We have to take this at heart when we compare the craving and urges of using drugs to the body natural desires for love and for food and water. To go without any of those for a certain length of time can be overwhelming and life threatening. That's why drug use in our society is a big burden and costs us in many different ways. I think even in the rise in health care costs, prisons being filled and family's broken up. SPIRITUAL maintenance would help in all these ordeals.

LETS TALK RECOVERY

What do we need to recover in our life? Many times when we are now getting our life back together, we feel we have to come up again in the financial world and get back our weight and muscles back in tack so we can look good. At this point we need to not self govern ourself and self sponsor ourself. We need to build a team to be responsible to. We do not need to worry about getting on our feet but getting on our knees. Try something new and different this time around. Any old crap we can give up we need to try to revamp our whole camp. Forget the outer wear and focus on the inner wear this time. To do the feel good and heal good. We have a dying need to recover our self-worth, our values and morals. Self dignity is a tool we use along with faith and a firm amount of determination can conquer any obstacles in our quest to get a grip on our life. The things we need to recover is not all material things at all, and real focus can land us in good standing on our come up. Feelings are key to success in our life and is a huge foundation to build on. Cars and clothes will not take us as far as compassion and a connection with our higher power. In the dope dealing world having a connect is big, in this spiritual world come back, a higher power connect is all important as well. This gives us the ability to give and receive love conditional and unconditional as well. Our kingdom will be in our own dome, and this kingdom will be built in inner higher places. It's nice to be in the right place at the right time. You are in the right place right now, so get it right right now. Those promises are true, we do recover.

BE WHAT YOU WANT TO BE

I say be who you want to be. I say learn who you are and be yourself. How do you see yourself? How do you think others see you, are they the same? You are not taking good stock of yourself until those two things equal almost the same or very near the same. The self inventory and self awareness is key to having self control as well as self esteem. Also to battle the self defeating charter defect of self centerness we must be able to take a real look at our self, not who we think we are, are who we want to be, but the true you/me. What you see is what you get, and to get the shot at getting on top, you will need to see it as it is and call it that way as well. One of the big difference in this over all view is how we look at our self and how we want others to see us, but which is more important, who you are compared to what you are. Who you are would be like you are a gentle caring person, what you are is like a soul singer and super model. The people that know who you are should have no problem loving you for you. When people chase you because you are a mega rap star, and not know the slightest bit who you are is a skin deep relationship. When you get to know yourself and make sure your partner know them self, the relationship will grow when the two of you began to learn about each other and God. To have a ego and be stuck on yourself is one of the things that can hold you back. We work on ridding the world of aids, hunger, and poverty, those are all honorable causes. When it comes to hunger its a two fold problem, lets tackle both. When Jesus tell his disciples to cast their nets on the other side of the boat when he tell them to feed his sheep. One is food for the body and one is soul food. We have too and need to do both as well. Feed my spirit and my body, feed my belly and my heart. Just as a living plant needs sunshine and rain to grow, they also need to be planted in good rich soil, where their roots can run deep. We as well need to be rooted and we grow from both joy and pain, like sunshine and rain. The winds and storms test our foundation and how well we are rooted.

The biggest tree on the up side do not stand, but the tree whose roots are dug down deep are the ones the weather the storms and winds that blow our way. The upper growth need the sunshine, the lower growth needs the rain. Both needs love nourishment running though their veins, to much of one will kill you. We need both in a health dose to be strong and live long. So goes life where we can see in animal life, plant life, life in the sea, or life in the sky, life is about more than you and I, and our life is not all about what we can be, as much as who we are meant to be. You be you and I will be me, we will share our life with all that live with thee. No matter what's the weather we are all is in this together, lets finds ways to make life better, yes life for you and life for me, even life for the apple tree. Things can be fun under the sun, resist the devil and he will run, together you and me can get things done. It takes two to tangle, and two parts to be whole, so lets feed both your body and soul, tree on top and roots on the bottom, stump on the devil and make him hollow. I got tired of him messing with me, now I learned resist thee and he will flee. The devil is two faced and I am on his case, in my life he can not win, show or place. To much I lost, his lies is a big cost, I got a new boss who carried his cross and blood he lost to pay that cost. When I got a new boss my life I thought I lost, but the peace I got, I wanted every one to have a piece. That's how it feel to be free and your old demons hold no more power over thee. Resist the devil and he will flee, resist craving and they will go away. resist temptations and you will get the miracles supreme. When we live though our spirit we are the love machine, you can be what you want to be on cloud nine, you can be who you want to be all the time. Apples for all, Real Talk, No Games, By James.

BACKWARDS THINKING

I speak much about these two worlds, I call them the 'spiritual and the flesh' or the material or the street life. The thing is I try to refer people to get into the spiritual world deeper and have less importance in the street life. It depends on which world you are in at the time that a certain way of thinking will be on key to a situation. In the street life people think of pimping as the cool title to have for their self. I tell you so many people got the pimping thinking to fit so many different understandings. I am from a big family and jealous feeling run deep. Many many people got this pimping thoughts backwards in my point of view. When some one think to dog a person out that they have hard core pimping skills and they are not weak. They think to have a heart is a tool for the weak pimps. I would not under stand why you would dog a person out and tear them down was pimping. Yes I under stand the control thing, but in business I think build a person up would be better so that we are able to lean on each other. They say get up on them and get out on them. No long term goals or plans for a partnership, that's all backward thinking to me and over all you are making someone a enemy that could of been a ally. All in the name of pimping, and its a big show thing to them as for as being seen doing some thing nice like holding hands is a gossip tool that say he is getting lovely dovly rather than having his foot on her back. Book pimping and looks pimping, to be a hard core pimp you must have full control and humiliate your gals. Not to get it twisted women pimp other women as well and do the book and look style too. Now we do know that the word pimp is used to state that you are feeling on top of your game. You got your car pimped out, meaning you got it fly and cool. Many people use the word I am pimping when they are doing some thing good that they are proud of, its just an expression. But we got the lost souls that do think its cool to pimp others, they call it white slavery. Black or white, slavery is not right, Red white and blue, pimping is wrong too. Many so called pimps judge other so called pimps as weak and/or fake. Oh by all means its many fake people out there regardless of the field they are in. Weak in my opinion is any one that feel the need to pimp another person. They are sick when they want to low rate another person. Its a sickness that has blinded them and have them in a web of self defeating habits and devilish thinking. On both ends of this relationship its sickness going on and they are both feeding each other in misery. At times people get caught up in this life style and they have no ideal how they got there. But the sickness progress and it becomes an addiction just as money can be, just as drugs can be. Life style is a deep well as well that can bind us into a life of bondage, we have to over come many demons in our battle for recovery. Life style is a huge one, drug addiction is a huge one as well. But they all feed off each other and when we try to cure one without understanding and dealing with the others its not curing the whole problem. Its a band aid cure. Mental illness, low self worth, drug addiction and alcoholism, negative life style and poverty, being a victim of violence or rape are some of the issues a person could have. We only see the drunk on the out side of the person but if we get deep in their soul, we would see the problem as a whole. Abandonment and let downs by love ones and society we get the second class view of our self and now the break though can be so messy when we do get into their spirit, we know that only the grace of God can lift this person back into first class thinking of their self. They have to own a purpose bigger than their own life now, they have to take a hold of Gods will and form new goals to go after, like being a blessing to others in life. Their new mission is one of selfless and seeking to help others and serve God and man kind. They need to see good in what they are doing and feel it. They have to want to spare others of the road and pain they endured. They become mighty in spirit. They reverse that pimp thinking to Gratitude and servitude attitude.

PIMPING BACKWARDS

So some think in terms of charm or being a gentleman pimp, a lover not a fighter. My over all point is that to think you need to pimp any one is backwards out here. To have the need to control others is in ways a weakness. To have self control gives you the power to succeed at any and many things. Again I refer to the book 'AS A MAN THINKET' by James Allen, he say self control is mastery. When you master your self you are calm and confident. With a strong spirit and the right attitude only god knows the limit of the things one can do. Then you connect to others that have this self control under control and you fellow ship or partner ship with the mighty in spirit and you encourage each other and support one another and the rich gets richer and the poor gets poorer. To have a poor spirit is to have a need to pimp are to destroy others spirit. You think when you break their spirit they are your slave, that's just how the devil thinks and those are the tools the devil use too. Snake moves like under the apple tree, deceive, divide, demoralize and try to have you believe they are god themselves, Willie Lynch had those moves and attitude as well. Pimping and that whole mind set with their stable, reminds me of the view Willie Lynch and his speech and his style of running his plantation. Oh yes in the street world you are the king, but how many lives do you lead away from god thinking you are god to them. That's not feeding Jesus sheep, that's leading them to the slaughter house, I do not believe god would like that. Lost in this fast rat race world you better find your self and get control of your self. What in the world are you thinking, why? Its many ways you can make this right in your mind, you label others. You lift your self to think you are better and above others. Then you label others, you stereotype them and then you attack and abuse them and you believe its ok. You call them half human, or whores and you justify it to abuse them. Just as pimps began to believe their above in this evil and misfortune, the others on the other side of this igorness also began

to believe and except the abuse. To be free you have to know that master /
slave or pimp / whore are all living in a sick and miseral bondage life wasting
circumstances. We saw it with the invasion of crack on our neighborhoods.
The deadly out come was hurtful on each corner of the box. The dealers
spread poison in the community. Families were baring the burden from all
fronts in their lives. It became another tool for the powers to be to label and
target the already confused people in the getthos. The getthos of their mind
and their community as well. This labeling made good for new target laws,
it made good for the media to label certain side of towns and streets, and
people. Just as gang life was media good ratings to produce shows like cops,
the drug life did make great showing as well. Now the crack law would clearly
affect the ones that are showed on corners and the label and stereotype all
would fit. The people on both sides of the issue would believe and accept
the abuse. Again to show how the labels allow for targeting and abuse to
be used and justified and accepted. People believe what they see and hear
and it allow them to hold on to their self righteous view that they are better
than the have nots. Then the low in self worth believe the world is against
them, they feel hopeless and as victims and they drown their problems in
the drugs. Now the whole gets the down hill pouring of this war on drugs
plus the drugs killing them too. They get it going and coming, then they
want to pimp and deal as a means of getting respect and livelihood. That's
the backwards thinking and the Willie Lynch bondage game plan. The slave
only see the master as a way of life to rely on, the whore the pimp, the dealer
the drugs. The drugs and alcohol is just a relief from the pain and to cope
with the hopeless, their truth is that they are the target of hate as well as
victims and in a pity party. They see the small dealer get the blame and the
prison game goes on where the have nots get had all over again. The crack
law say it all, as do the show cops on where the focus, the labeling, the hoods
where the hunting game is in play. What you going to do when they come
for you? Watch your spirit, protect your heart. The devil is always roaming
seeking to kill, steal and destroy. What you going to do when they come for
you. Get the drugs out of your pockets and out of your system, alcohol and
drugs is a tool the devil use to destroy you and our community too. Drugs
and alcohol kill in more ways than one. They kill they spirit and they are the
bad apples on the tree. No crying when the cops get you because drugs are
a tool the enemy use on you. Drugs is in kids system when they kill some
one in a senseless death. We can not leave it to the cops to fix this problem,
they do it from a legal point of view, and they have too, its a need for that
too. But its a greater need for the apple tree movement to deal with the

drugs and this message to the gangs. The apple for all is to lift spirits which is the real answer to dealing with all these problems. No one gets the blame for the problem, we are all to be held to a share of fixing the problem by supporting this apple for all movement.

WORLDS AT WAR

Now to pimp your car out or create this word to show your style in fashion, we get that. That's why I say pimping holds so many views and meaning to many people. I just want the understanding of the two worlds and the worlds is at war too, THE SPIRIT AND THE FLESH WORLD. I think the spirit world will win in the end. I know the street world holds some huge temptations and that it's a world that must exist too. The thing that becomes a great problem is when you have no regard for the spiritual world and you will do anything for the almighty dollar. That's selling your soul to the devil in many ways. The devil rules this world so we must learn to be in this world but not of that world. That's why in the bible they say the ruler of this world is always roaming seeking to kill, steal and destroy. That's why in the bible they say that God say a friend of this world is not a friend of mines. That's why the bible say be in this world but not of this world. I can go on and on and on about the two worlds, but in the cartoons in Hollywood motion pictures you see when someone die their body go down in the dirt but the spirit rise high to the sky. I am not saying that everyone that has done some so called pimping is evil, the action was evil but the spirit was caught up in these worlds at war. Turmoil in your soul, and in the bible they say wars come from the flesh at odds with the spirit. That's how I got that message given. My message is that it's wrong to abuse people in the name of pimping, or in the name of religion. God gave gifts and some were teachers, preachers, encouragers, prophets, no mention of pimps that I seen. No one has all the answers, and government has its powers and its laws and its needs, but the spiritual world has its laws as well. Some times issues take on a life of their own, such as health care bill. Now we need not look for blame or go to finger pointing on drug issues, its a fight that court laws can not solve alone. It is just as complex as any issue we ever faced in this nation. Moral and spiritual outlooks has to play a part in this as a whole. What kind of war is it, by the people for the people. I speak on this issue out of passion, its the strongest cause I center my foot in, apples for addicts and alcoholics. You see I related this book by cartoones, songs, pimping, slavery and above all God. The twists and turns some will relate to and others will not, crime from both sides of the coin. If I can just get the spark lit it will raise the stakes and take on a life on its own. I do believe that this is also not just saving the soul of an addict, it will roll up hill. It will save one man, one child, then a family, a neighborhood and so on. We will save apple trees or whole communitys, up hill battle in courts. This will not be in police power or mans power, this war for liberty in the two worlds will have to be won in the spiritual world first and for most. This is why I am calling people out in the name of the first fruit, the apple to set us on fire. God gave adam the first man, whom we all came from the whole garden and choice of free will. Man can only give and take so much of freedom, other freedom comes from within and spirit is in the hands of no man. That world God has in his hands and some of our problems we have to lay at his feet and then have faith, conceive, believe and achieve the freedom, freedom from dugs and stinking thinking. Live life more abundant and less stressful. Every man will seek to be equal in self control. Yes if all men seek to be equal in self control, we will see a world that we all can get alone. Its to many religion wars, and since its nearly impossible to all get alone in this world where our feet walks on dirt, can we all pick up our shield of faith and seek to be equal in self control. There fore not having the need to control, enslave, pimp, police others. When we feed the sheep and become lamb like we will get one world to all get alone in, see no blame in and be equal in. We all will have self worth and self control, jealous reason will not have value, as money in this world will be none void as well. This is a different world for sure and crazy it sounds, but oh so wonderful it looks in my vision. I hope in this apple movement Gods shepards come forth. Self help is where all men can make a huge difference, one at a time, one day at a time. One life at a time, in this life here and now, because we were all kids somewhere in a different life.

LA LA LAND

Walking with a limp or dressed flashy all claim the name of pimped out. We have a whole line of brothers that went crazy with the pimping in their mind. They claimed and believed in a false god they named the pimp god. That they really for real looked to as their higher power, and they were crazy as hell on the real. Walking and talking to themselves, lost and their ability to hold a normal conversation was gone to the land of la la, lost angels, living angry, angry at the world for not seeing their pink thinking. Pink caddie with rock stars calling them daddy. But on the real to see them consumed with pimping and they are in need of the first crazy house and the biggest pill to get them back with us in these two worlds, because they are in a whole different world out in the land of the lost. Pimping has run many many crazy that way, I guess to abuse your spirit to that level the world of la la is for the lost that can not be found. But is anything to hard for God? Let your spirit soar, do not try to bind it like your whore. Get that man mad like popeye saying I have taken all I can take and I ain't taken no more. Humans get sore and keep score unlike Jesus where 70 x 70 he can bore. Glory be for you and for me, I think we are all in need of grace, surely if we get caught up in this rat race. That world can make a zero look like a hero but we know that it's only a show that's all for show. It's a different world than where we come from. We may have been in that world but we are not of that world, when we dig deep in our mind we will see. When we mine our spirit we dig the gold out for the golden rule, our spirit rule, Gods armor we will use.

SELF SAVE FROM SELF

The turmoil from the wars within. Can we make inner peace with our self. They say wars cost a lot, yes the wars do. They cost us self worth and battles with our own love one. We turn friends to foes, not to mention the damage and pain we do to our spirit. Then comes the pain meds and addiction issues and/or p.t.s. Words we put into our spirit is part of training and exercise to prepare us for the war. Part of this war is to get control, self control. In wars we do need to blow up bridges, the ones that lead to bars or drug houses. Also in the german war the wall was built for a purpose, the wall did that job but it did harm also, we have to weigh the pros and cons. We may have to huff and puff and blow that wall down. We have to take self inventory to see what we need to win this war, and what we do not need that is in our way of our self. There are always need for changes, our main thing in us is the need to change our thinking. We also need to be open minded rather than closed minded. As beauty is only skin deep, most shadow people are only concern with the outter appearance. Clothes does not make the man, you are not what you wear, you are what you think. Some people feel self worth when they are dressed in fine gear, or when they are driving a lincon, that's just stinking thinking. You want to put jewelry on to look and feel good, but you are a diamond in the rut, dig in your spirit and mine your mind and soul. Take that stone hard heart put pressure on it and knock off the dirty parts and polish it, your heart is a jewel, its an emerald, you are a diamond in the rut. The beauty is in you, not on you, save you, jim is a gem.

PUSH

Don't push me I'm close to the edge, im trying not to lose my head. A person that's drinking and using alcohol, their life can be like a jungle. My life was like a jungle and I had to wonder how I would keep from going under. For me the answer to that question was and is god. I ask you to ask your self that same question, how and why are you still here. How did you make it past the rats and roaches and the junkies with the base ball bats. Did god have a purpose for you? Why not try gods will for you rather than the will you have for yourself. When we are using drugs and drinking we are close to the edge. No one needs to push us because we will likely go over all by our self unless we save our self and make some changes in our life. We are on a slippery icy road with bald tires and the edge is running out of guard rails. We do ourself worst than any one else do us. Remember crack killed apple jack, he jumped in but could not jump back. Don't push that pipe, don't push your luck just push the basket so I do not have to carry your casket. Crack kills, program member's lives. In our fight with our self to stay sober is like push and pull or tug of war. The flesh against the spirit and our will against the all powerful drug cravings. Thus where our sanity is concerned and nerves on edge we need no one pushing us to use. Take a drink to calm your nerves and take off the edge is a push that a addict does not need. Since crack killed apple jack and he jumped in and could not jump back, we do not need no push like that. For a fien to stay clean he must keep his life centered and not near the edge. Don't push me. At the turning point treatment center back in the days we were encouraged to keep each other on our toes. So when you confront others in the program we would approach them and say "let me pull you up" on what ever the issue was that you saw a need to talk to them about. Say if they were cursing a lot, I would say let me pull you up on your language. We saw that as reaching out to our family member. We all looked at each other as family, and to pull each other up was keeping each other on our toes and in check as well. Not to pull each other down as crabs in a barrel, but to pull each other up as family and community relatives. In the big cities its like the jungle where rules for survival is an accuse to do deviless things and pull others down to get your self up. When some one go over the edge you push them over and do a victory dance with your arms in the sky. Not I, no no not to day, no way no how. Those are not the rules we use, that's not the way of the games we play. My greeting cards label is named "REAL TALK—NO GAMES, BY JAMES" so we keep it real these days, we are not about hating, we are about "PULL UPS" not the crab barrel pull down attitude. Don't push me cause I am close to the edge. If you are over the edge, hang on, it will not be long before the helping hands people come to your aid, they do it without getting paid. Even though their life is centered, they hang around the edge so they can lend a helping hand. They reached the turning point in their life and that impact from turning point stayed with them and me to this very day, we still want unity in our community. We did our share of doing damage in the streets, and now we want and need to give back. We want to pull you up if you are on the edge. It comes a point when you have to turn your life around, have you reached that turning point? Turning point will pull you up, eden house will pull you up, Fair view will pull you up, st. joes will pull you up. Minneasota and their treatment centers will pull you up, we have some of the best in the whole wide world. Hazelton, St. Marys and also teen challenge are among the helping hands people that will help you to turn your life around, and there are many many more. They do not push, they pull, they do not pull the wool over your eyes. They pull you up in spirit and help you to turn your life around. You can do it, we know you can and we are willing to give you a helping hand. We will not push, but we are pulling for you. Can I pull you up, will you pull your fiends up? Its never to late to turn your life around. Crack killed apple jack, he jumped in but could not jump back. Apple jack we got your back, apple jack' apple for addicts is where its at. When you can't jump back, we will pull you up, we will pull for you. Its the turning point, so you can rock around the apple tree. Apple jack our apple tree stands for unity in the community. Apples for addicts and alcoholics. Apple jack you are not boxed in, you have a friend, apples for all will not let you fall. Apple jack we know crack kills, but we are having none of that, apples for all is doing some out of the box thinking. Crack kills, but that's not our will, apple jack, one bad apple don't spoil the hole bunch, Minneasota is not out to lunch. Not in the treatment field, we do not yield, we are on the case. My kids will eat apple jacks for lunch or captain crunch, alcoholics and addicts love their kids a whole bunch. So don't push me.

WHY NOT WHAT

It's easier for people to forgive you for what you have done if they understand why you have done it. It's kind of like a guy in court and plead guilty with a explanation. You too can forgive yourself if you understand that your addiction left you powerless over your values and decision making process. What you do is not as important as why you do something, good or bad. Do you make the coffee or put a dollar in the basket to be seen, or to give back? Why are you sober? What good will it do you and others? We know what a heart is but why do we have it? PRAYER—Lord help me watch my why's. Why did I want to write a book apples for addicts? It would give me a chance to feed the sheep as Jesus asked his disciples to do. I wanted to be shepard for a cause and to be a part of something helpful to others. I wanted to bring the same things to you but in a different way. It's not so much what I have in these pages as to why I have them in there. I wanted to speak the language of many people and touch anyone that lifts this book to read. I wanted to bring some funny ways of telling these stories, and I wanted to give the spirit a view that we can use it in a simple way without the holier than thou attitude. I want to bring God to you as a higher power that's able to come to us on our level and really be a difference maker in our lives. Most of all I wanted to get you to believe in you and see that your thinking has the power to control your life and take you where you desire to be, and spirit is a tool to use for your betterment in life.

9 781453 545508